ADVANCE PRAISE

"O'NEAL SHOWS US A WAY toward healing through wild courage, trust, and commitment. We all have access to a beautiful life, even after trauma, despair, and heartbreak. *She Rides Wild Horses* infuses us with the inspiration to thrive, not just survive."

—Jenny Carr, best-selling author of *Peace of Cake*

"WITH COURAGE AND HONESTY, Jess Camilla O'Neal weaves a real-life adventure story that spans the spectrum from funny to tear-jerking, spirited to nearly-broken, tragedy to triumph, and so much in between. *She Rides Wild Horses* is a raw, yet beautiful, testimony to Jess's indomitable spirit and tough-as-nails attitude, and the depth of the experiences that tried to break her, yet instead strengthened her spirit. Inspiring and entertaining, the well-told stories of this real-life Wyoming cowgirl who found healing through horses, music, love, and a stubborn refusal to give up, offers fresh insight into the capacity of the human spirit to soar even while the body struggles to heal."

—Lisa Wade Berry, best-selling author of
*Real. Big. Love. A Difference Maker's Guide
to Gain Greater Clarity, Energy, and Impact
for Your Cause and Life*

Blaze,

She Rides
Wild Horses

May you Always
Ride Wild Horses

She Rides
Wild Horses

The Rugged, Real-Life Story
of an Unbreakable Woman

BY JESS CAMILLA O'NEAL

UN-SETTLING BOOKS
Boulder, Colorado USA

ISBN: 978-1-7330145-7-1

Music rights:

Someone Else's Story
By Benny Anderson, Bjorn Ulvaeus, and Tim Rice
Copyright Universal Polygram International Publishing, Inc.
ADMINISTERED BY HAL LEONARD

Whatcha Gonna Do With a Cowboy
By Garth Brooks and Mark D. Sanders
Copyright Major Bob Music, Inc. and Mid-Summer Music, Inc.
ADMINISTERED BY 50% Major Bob, Wendi Crosby York

The Change
By Tony Arata and Wayne Tester
Copyright Universal Music Corp. o/b/o McA Music Publ., A.D.O. Univer,
Universal Music Corp. o/b/o Forerunner Music Inc., and Words, and Music
Copyright Admn o/b/o Little Tybee Music
ADMINISTERED BY HAL LEONARD

Cover and Content Design: Sally Wright Day
Editing: Maggie McReynolds
Author Photo: Sky Garnick

For those who have been afraid to tell their truth
For those who have been brave enough to rise above
Keep moving, keep doing, keep loving

Contents

Prologue xi

Chapter One: She Rides 1

Chapter Two: Trouble in Paradise 21

Chapter Three: Becoming 39

Chapter Four: Leap of Faith 51

Chapter Five: Chrysalis 79

Chapter Six: Trail or Trial 89

Chapter Seven: Heartbreak and Horses 105

Chapter Eight: Life with a Rockstar 117

Chapter Nine: Daddy Issues 141

Chapter Ten: The Wake 157

Chapter Eleven: Paper Bullets of the Brain 167

Acknowledgments 183

About the Author 184

Thank You 185

Prologue

You can't stop her from dreaming
Can't tell her when she's done
She's a good old hand she'll outwork any man
She is bright like the sunshine and cool as the moon
and she rides wild horses for fun.

~ "She Rides Wild Horses,"
by Jess Camilla O'Neal

The chill wind was harsh on this Halloween night. It whistled through the shattered windshield as I slammed my foot on the gas pedal, ducked below the steering wheel, and sped off blindly. Bullets whizzed behind my head and my neck. My cheek was still warm from a bullet that graciously missed my head. Was I alive or dead?

There was broken glass everywhere. I spat it from my mouth, brushed it off my face, and wiped it away from my eyes. My blood surged through my veins and pulsed with every rapid heartbeat. I couldn't make sense of what was left or right, up or down, real or imaginary.

Adrenaline. This was not my first hypnotic taste of this self-made drug, and this was not my first brush with death. I was very familiar with this sensation, comfortable in this ethereal in-between state. A man had just stood point blank in front of my truck, looked me in the eye, and shot at me. Why? Why now, after all that had transpired? How much heartbreak can a human endure? How does the heart heal from so much betrayal?

I truly thought my time of suffering had ended. After my parents lost the family ranch, a traumatic fall at age 17 had shattered both my legs, and I was told I'd never walk again. Ten years later, I lost my father to an unexpected heart attack. I felt I had learned enough from the Universe. Yet here I was with everything shattering around me, the broken windshield a perfect metaphor for my existence.

What then transpired was like every movie scene you've ever watched: time stood still, slow-motion action resumed, and what was supposed to be a minute became a montage of memories. Scenes of my short-lived life of 30 years played out before me. Captivated by my own stories of love, loss, trial, and joy, I surrendered to the suffering.

Was this my final moment of transformation? Before me was the epitaph of my previous life. I was at the doorstep, knocking at my own come-to-Jesus meeting. This moment was now mine. Despite the danger and the odds, I made my choice to wake up and live.

CHAPTER 1:

She Rides

Music.
Horses.
Laughter.
Tragedy.
Family.
Wyoming.

Those are bullet points in the timeline of my short, yet eventful, life. Words that truly meld my spirit to this realm. They are not in any particular order, but they carry equal weight.

The Ranch

My family owned Heart Six dude ranch just north of Jackson Hole, Wyoming, and six miles from the entrance to Grand Teton and Yellowstone national parks. We also owned and operated a live theatre in downtown Jackson Hole.

As a little girl, I spent my days with my seven siblings, running, jumping, and racing my horse in the dark woods of Bridger Teton National Forest. By night, my imagination flourished in the costume attic of the dark, prop-cluttered wings at the edge of the small stage of our historic live theatre.

My love of animals began quite young. My mom would watch *Lifestyles of the Rich and Famous* on TV as she mindlessly took care of household chores. From the first time I heard host Robin Leach's distinctly nasal English accent raving over the most indulgent homes and yachts on the planet, I knew with every fiber of my being, that I was destined to be (imagine the English accent here) a rich and famous pig fah-meh. My dreams were so close to coming to fruition. I already had pigs, so I only needed to become rich and famous. Totally doable—especially for a four-year-old.

As I grew, I continued to hold pigs in high regard, but I soon discovered horses. Once horses entered the picture, every thought of raising pigs melted quickly away. My new goal was to become rich and famous by way of anything equine. In 1984, my parents bought me a beautiful, old, flea- bit, gray gelding with a reddish mane and tail. I called him Apple after my favorite My Little Pony character. I spent every waking minute trying to ride him, and if I was asleep, I was dreaming of him. Every day, I begged my dad to take me to the corrals. If Dad wouldn't take me, I'd venture out alone, which would send my parents on a wild, frantic chase looking for me. They almost always found me hanging off the rough poles of the corral, seeking my equine friends. Horses heal the soul, give wings to the spirit, and bring freedom to the mind. Even at this very young age, I was drawn to their magnificence, beauty, and power. Honestly, I wanted to be one.

When I wasn't pretending to be a horse, I was atop my trusty steed. Apple taught me strength, courage, and trust. He was magnificent, my knight in shining armor in white horse form. I was around six when I was finally able to scope him out in the herd of 150 head of horses, jump off the edge of the fence and grab the nearest halter, toss the lead rope over his neck as he tried to escape, and lead him out of the horse poo that was ankle-deep in the corral and over to the hitching rail, where I had schemed up an incredible saddling system that I could accomplish all by myself.

Stepping into the dusty, low-lit saddle shed was like stepping 100 years back in time. There was only a single window that cast a sepia-toned hue through dust-scattered sunbeams over the 100 or more saddles we used to make the dude ranch run. The pungent scent of old, oiled leather, sweaty horse blankets, and strong rusted iron from used horse shoes was so evocative it could elicit vivid memories from any horseperson from anywhere in the world. Saddle sheds all smell the same. Once you've known the smell, it will entice you for all eternity.

There, hanging off the lowest saddle rack, was a small, plain, light brown saddle with "#2" written on the kind of ear tag for tagging cattle, but in this case used for keeping track of all the ranch saddles. I knew #2 was mine to use. I would reach on my tippy-toes to the saddle horn and

3

pull with all my six-year-old might, slamming it down onto my hip as I stood sideways in perfect form to catch it there. The flopping stirrups and dragging saddle strings left tracks in the fine dust that collected on the wooden slab floor no matter how many times we swept. I'd drag the heavy saddle out to the porch and then to the hitching rail where Apple patiently waited. Setting the saddle with its pommel tipped up, I'd strategically scoot an old stump that sat by the door, rocking it side to side until it was close to Apple's side, then hop off the porch and scurry under his belly to smooch and push him until his broad side was against the rail. Some days, when Apple was feeling his oats, I had to repeat this process three or four times.

Then I'd step onto the stump, grab the heavy saddle, and inch it up my legs until my left hand was under the horn and my right hand under the back skirt. With a one-two-three, I'd simultaneously give a little jump and try to heave the saddle onto Apple's back. If I did it right, I'd land on the ground and make my way around him, pulling the strings on each side to jockey the saddle right into the sweet spot. Then back under his belly I'd go, cinching the saddle up tight and securing it with a knot to his back. It was quite a lot of effort for a small kid.

Apple was a very kind, loving horse, but he was old and knew a lot of tricks, so bridling him, which came next, called for a little more coercion. I'd grab a little handful of grain from the bin, climb along the rail like a cat, and then perch next to his head and offer him a little snack. When he came in for a bite, I'd swoop the bit into his mouth and the bridle over his ears, all while balancing on the porch rail.

Some days I'd fall and eat a lot of dirt while getting Apple ready to ride. Other days it would go more smoothly, and once I'd saddled him and tightened the reins, I could jump and land first my left knee, and then my left foot, into the stirrup closest to the rail, stand up straight, and swing my tiny right leg over his back. He was so broad that it felt like I was doing the splits to ride him, but I loved every minute of it. With the quick slap on his butt from my reins, we were off, wild and free and exploring the trails behind our ranch.

One particular spring day, I decided to ride with some guests from the ranch. The creeks and bogs were swollen with winter run-off, and I was riding in the very back and taking the job of tail gunner very seriously. I could hear our trail wrangler, on whom I had a tiny crush, up front, where he hollered to the guest behind him, "Now, your horse might jump this bog, just hang tight to your saddle horn and stay in the middle!"

Here, clearly, was my chance to have some fun. I held Apple back and waited until everyone had crossed the bog and was out of sight. Then I kicked him up so he was running—I wanted to get a big jump out of him. In my head, I was Elizabeth Taylor in National Velvet (if you haven't seen the movie, binge it right after reading this book). Apple, of course, was Pie, the award-winning jumper from the movie. We picked up more speed. Apple leaned back to get a big jump, and we were airborne! But as we were soaring, I noticed that my view of the horizon

5

was starting to shift. The horizon was no longer above me, and my view was no longer of trees and sky but of hooves and mud.

Somehow, during our big launch, my saddle had slipped, and I was hanging for dear life to Apple's underbelly. With every downbeat of his back hooves, he stepped on my beautiful, long, blonde ponytail and pulled my head back. I was young enough to find this wildly entertaining, and I giggled uncontrollably as we whizzed by the rest of the folks on the trail ride.

The worried wrangler ran after us and caught Apple, yelling at me to let go. I did, plopping out from under my horse and into yet another muddy bog. I got up and brushed as much mud off me as I could. My tall cowboy crush fixed my saddle upright, and away we went again happily down the trail.

I considered this day a rousing success.

Apple was the finest of horses, the perfect companion for an eager little cowgirl. Not once did he spook nor step on me. Not once did he betray my trust, or me his. We were soulmates, and I loved him dearly. But I was grew older, so did he, and as time passed, he could no longer jump the logs and muddy bogs. I wanted to be fast and ride in the rodeos, but he was ready for greener pastures.

One heartbreaking afternoon, my father came to me and told me that Apple had passed on. I was hysterical.

"No, Dad! I want to see him!"

"He's gone, honey."

"Please, Dad."

"You sure?"

I was sobbing outright. "Yes!"

"Alright, honey-girl, but he is no longer there, and it will be hard," Dad said.

This was my first knowing of loss. Dad took me to see his body. There on the corral floor lay my friend, his white hide contrasting against the dark, wet, mineral-rich earth, his reddish mane fanned out against the dirt. His legs were splayed as if he was running, running away from this life into the next, fast into his new summer pastures of eternity. I crumpled across his back, touching my teary wet cheek to his skin. A little warmth was left in his soft hide, but it soon faded to cold as I sat and sobbed. I could feel Dad by my side. I stayed there whimpering, letting it all out. I didn't like to cry in front of Dad, but when I looked up, my father had tears streaming down his cheeks too. I knew then we both were changed by the love of this sweet horse. He was my favorite horse. As they all have been.

After Apple passed away, it was several years before I had my very own horse. I could, of course, ride any horse I wanted to out of our dude string, but that wasn't the same as having my own companion. I begged my parents for my own horse, but they had just started a huge ranching business. We had enough horses, so one from the herd would have to do for a while.

I often slept with my windows cracked open to catch the crisp, fragrant mountain air. One summer morning, I heard the soft whinnying of a horse luring me to and from my dreams with its excited, metronomic tones.

Faintly, I heard my father's deep, resonant voice.

"Jessie, honey, wake girl, wake up. I have a present for you."

As I rubbed sleep from my eyes, I saw, below my second-story window, my handsome dad holding a halter rope. On the other end of that rope was the most beautiful, slick, sorrel mare I had ever seen, her wild mane and tail dancing back and forth. I jumped out the window onto the sloping roof, the tin already warm from morning sun against my bare legs. I slid off gently into my dad's long, strong arms as he lifted me onto my mare's back. I could feel her withers quivering and her coarse hair against my calves. Never before had I felt so tall, so big, so proud!

"What are you going to name her?" Dad asked me as he gently looped her halter rope around her proud neck to make me a quick rein. This gorgeous steed was obviously Tinkerbell. I could feel her sass, speed, and temperament in the first seconds of our meeting. Gracefully, my dad swung up behind me, using only Tinkerbell's mane. "Give her a kick," he said.

With the lightest touch of my heel, Tinkerbell, Dad, and I loped onto the dew-kissed meadow near the banks of the Buffalo Fork River. This would become a cherished memory, one of the greatest days of my life. I felt so much joy, love, and peace being with my first loves, Dad and my horses, all of them the gateway to my equine addiction.

My childhood days at the ranch were perfect. I was free to do as I pleased: ride, swim, and join the other children in daily activities such as hikes, scavenger hunts, and target practice with bow and arrows or black powder rifles. I mostly chose to ride.

By the time I was eight, my father had taught me about the edible plants that surrounded us, and I'd become entranced by and knowledgeable of both the flora and fauna that shared our playground, the Bridger Teton National Forest. It was not unusual to see a grizzly bear scavenging down the same trail we used to race to our friends' houses on our ponies. Herds of elk, deer, and buffalo were common sights on our outings. Respect for nature and our surroundings was imprinted onto us as deeply as our daily scripture study, an integral part of the Mormon religion in which we were raised.

The ancient horse and wild game trails known to the Indians were the gateway to all of our adventures. My older sister Vanessa and I were the fairy queens of Buffalo Valley. I woke very early most mornings, before the touch of dawn graced the peaks of the Grand Tetons hovering over our dude ranch. I could hear the call of the sandhill cranes as I made the ten-minute walk to our corrals, and the faint humming of the electric fence our neighbor had erected to keep our horses from munching on his flowers.

I walked up the steep steps of the ranch bunkhouse, jumping the weird half-step that the carpenters failed to scale properly (my father cursed that step daily, as it frequently sent some unknowing guest careening down the stairs, twisting ankles and knees and taking down anyone in its path). In the bunkhouse, amidst the ripe smell of horse shit, sweaty horse blankets, sour teenage-boy socks, and scattered Copenhagen cans filled with tobacco spit, lived the most handsome cowboys—the collective crushes of my youth. These were the wranglers who worked for us, young men eager to spend their summer days away from the tedium that was the rest of the ranch work, of putting up hay and irrigating, trading all that for a chance to guide people in the mountains and a chance at a much more western cowboy social life.

I sat patiently on the stoop until I heard the cowboys start to stir, and the stomping of boots, jingling of spurs, cussing, laughter, and groans as they readied for the day. Then the day truly began with the catching, brushing, and saddling of 100 head of horses set to the urging melodies of Chris Ledoux, Garth Brooks, the Judds, Tanya Tucker, and George Straight. The soundtrack of our everyday lives.

The Theatre

In the summer of 1978, two years before I was born, my mother Vicki was only 23, with a baby on her skinny hip and a dream larger than the Wyoming sky to open her own live theatre. She and my father had met while performing at Robert Redford's summer theatre at his resort, Sundance. My parents fell madly, deeply in love at first sight.

My mom had been raised in the sheltered Mormon culture of Orem, Utah, and this was her first taste of a real cowboy and the wild west. I believe it was my dad's sense of adventure and passion that attracted her to him, and my mother's beauty and goodness that attracted him to her. I'm sure it helped that they were both intensely beautiful humans. They were a perfect, fiery match—a power couple. Dad had been bitten by the acting bug in college. He was a tall, handsome guy, and he began to enjoy some success in Hollywood getting cast in low-budget films, commercials, and even some Clint Eastwood flicks. But eventually the traffic, tall buildings, and sheer number of other humans got to this Wyoming cowboy. He and Mom wanted more for each other and their family, so they left LA and went back to make Jackson Hole their home.

My father's parents, Bill and Billie, were never too far behind Dad. So together the four of them found a resort lodge up in the boonies of northwestern Wyoming called Brooks Lake Lodge. They endured the long, harsh winter, with the only access to the lodge being by snowmobile. I remember Dad telling us that the snow was so deep you could snowmobile over the roofs, and that once, when he gone to Jackson for supplies, Mom was snowed in with their firstborn for two days. If my mother had been looking for a true wild west adventure, she'd found one.

But things weren't working out for them at Brooks Lake. The land was on a forest service lease, and buying that lease out meant redoing the entire septic system, something they couldn't afford. Time to regroup. Dad and Grandpa Bill had found outfitting permits up for sale that would allow them to guide hunters on national forest land and suit their vision of making a living in as close to a cowboy lifestyle as they could, but with better wages. In the meantime, Mom had heard there was a building that had been used as a concert hall available to rent. She'd always wanted to run and operate her own live theatre. While Dad travelled south to try and book some hunting trips, Mom tried to figure out how to come up with the $22,000 she needed for a down payment on the building.

She landed on an unconventional idea. She gathered up all the alcohol from the bar at Brooks Lake Lodge, and took it to a Jackson-area cowboy bar to sell. They bought some of the inventory, and so did the next bar. Encouraged, Mom visited a few other local watering holes, winding up at a joint called Spirits of the West. In her perfectly coifed do and her pink maternity outfit (she was five months pregnant with me), she drew herself up and asked if they would like to purchase some liquor. "I have some very nice, expensive-looking bottles," she said proudly. "And these bottles here in the purple bags look cute. I have lots of different items. I have a whole truck full I need to get rid of!"

"Young lady," the man behind the counter said. "Excuse me. You have what?"

"I have some alcohol for sale," she repeated "I have a dream to start a live theater here in town. My family and I are LDS, and we will never drink or use this stuff, so I thought I could sell it to help me out."

"Vera Cheney's theatre? Good luck," the man said sarcastically under his breath.

Mom was undeterred. "Well, I just need to raise this money so I can try."

"Young lady," he said, raising an eyebrow, "show me how much alcohol you have." Mom took him out to the truck where she had the rest of the liquor stashed.

He looked it all over. "Do you know that what you are doing is illegal?"

Mom was shocked.

"Oh my, no. I had no idea. I promise."

The man looking at her up and down in all her pink-suited naiveté. "The selling of alcohol without a liquor license is a federal offense. You can't do this."

Mom was crushed. As she started to leave, the man stopped her and wrote out a check for $8,000. As he handed it to her, he said, "I'm the liquor commissioner here in Teton county and I'll buy the rest of the inventory from you if you promise you will never do something like this again, and never tell anyone that I did this for you."

"Of course! I promise, never. Thank you, thank you so much!"

Mom had been raised deep in the Mormon church. She had no idea that selling (i.e., bootlegging) alcohol on the streets was illegal or, for that matter, much about the stock she was selling. The commissioner showed her some grace that day. Between that and Dad selling two hunting trips, my parents had just enough money to put a down payment on the lease of the Jackson Hole Playhouse, a town institution she opened in 1978 and that our family still runs today.

The Playhouse is in a beautiful Victorian building of some historic significance in Jackson. It's seen years of different business ventures: a stable, a house of ill repute, an automotive garage, and, finally, a concert hall and then a live theatre. The oldest standing building in Jackson Hole, its deeply rooted history is such an integral

13

part of my family that all of us children feel we'd have no creativity, character, or shape without it.

My first job as a professional actress was at age six, when I played Marta in *The Sound of Music*. I still remember my first line: "I'm Marta and I'm nine years old and I want a pink parasol." I performed this show nightly for 90 days during the summer of 1987. Vanessa and my younger sister, Savanna, were both in the show with me. That summer we learned the incredible value of theatre and what it means to show up every day, even if you don't feel like it.

On one occasion, my two sisters and I had been at the pool all day with the rest of the cast. We'd forgotten to put on sunscreen, and by performance time that evening, we were burnt to a crisp. There was one very fast costume change involving all three of us that had us crying in pain as our dresses were removed and our new costumes popped on. I remember the costume assistants wiping our tears and saying, "Now smile girls!" as they sent us back onstage to finish the show. That is one thing that I learned at a very young age: The show must go on.

A theatre family engenders a kind of closeness with other humans. What's interesting and significant to me is that I felt that kind of camaraderie with those I spent time in the mountains with as well. Both experiences require eating, sleeping, and working alongside others, though in very different ways, and they afford very similar life lessons. In the theatre, the vulnerability, the shared laughter and struggle, were things I was exposed to from every side at a very young age, creating in me a powerful desire to connect to others as well as a passion for performance. Isn't it every little girl's dream to be on stage, in the spotlight, getting dressed up in costumes and putting on makeup?

Actually, I really wasn't that into the costumes and makeup, but I loved performing for and meeting people. I loved the applause, the laughter, the cries, the sighs, and the oohs and ahhhs. I knew that I was taking these audiences with me on a journey, and that we were all escaping whatever reality we were facing for the moment. My imagination flourished, and I was encouraged to let it soar. Growing up in cowboy culture meant there wasn't always the time or space for communication of feelings. That was where music and theatre came in for me—a place to put my emotions out in the open. My inhibitions melted away under the hot stage lights. I loved to sing. I was born to sing. Performing has continued to be an integral part of my professional and spiritual aspect of my existence.

In the years that followed, life moved easy. The grass was green, tall, and plentiful. In the summer months, my family worked hard running the ranch by day and running the theatre by night. Then the chill of September crept in as a shimmering veil of frost on each stalk of golden grass and on every dying leaf of the deciduous trees. Slowly, the bugling elk made their way down the long trail to their winter feeding grounds. Bears roamed and foraged for their winter sustenance. September marked my birthday month, my own time of rebirth and growth.

In the fall, Dad guided hunters, and, if I was lucky,

I'd get to miss several weeks of the first quarter of school to be out in the wild with him. I learned how to pack a mule string, cook meals over a campfire, and to manage the inner workings of making life happen on horseback 50 miles from civilization, deep in the backwoods of the Wyoming wilderness. There, the spaciousness of impending winter is like a calm and steady breath. When it arrived and the snow came, my world was shrouded in its white hush, a reminder to slow down, reflect, and be still. Each passing season had its challenges, joys, and comforting repetitive tasks.

Music

Starting about the time I was nine years old, my three sisters (Vanessa, then 11, Savanna, age seven, and Rachael, then five) formed a professional singing group. We'd grown up singing together in church and in shows at our theatre. We learned very early on how to harmonize, and we were good at four-part harmony. On our long family road trips, we would listen to The Judds, lots of 1950s-era music like The Andrews Sisters, and pretty much every musical theatre soundtrack that had ever existed. Savanna and I, in particular, could always find the harmony, and we'd sing for hours on those drives. We would travel to the dude rancher conventions (yes, they exist!), which were usually held in Arizona. It was a vacation, but it was also work for us kids. We got hired locally for parties and other events, and during the holidays we would dress up in old-timey caroling outfits and get hired to sing carols. Some of those performances were really humbling, but as we grew older, the gigs got bigger. My parents had big ambitions for us; they wanted us to be more than a local attraction—in fact, they wanted us to have national careers. For a time—and I'll tell more about this as we go—we even did.

4-H

The Garnicks were big on 4-H. Every child in our household had a 4-H project, whether it was raising steers, sheep-shearing, hog handling, sewing, or showing horses. Like my siblings, I pledged my head to clearer thinking, my heart to greater loyalty, my hands to greater service, and my health to better living. This was the mantra of our weekly meetings, the pledge of any member of the 4-H club. The words didn't evoke much emotion in me when I was young, but as I grew older and came to understand the weight of these words, I came to believe that this way of being is an honorable one.

Our level of involvement was ridiculously intense. One year, we had five steers and three sheep showing in the Teton County fair. We lived about 40 miles from town at the time, so we had to haul enough water, feed, and showing equipment for a week. We didn't have enough space in the horse trailers for the sheep, but my grandparents had a 1980 mustard yellow station wagon complete with wood panel interior—just what anyone would think of as the perfect livestock transport!

After fair week, my sister, two friends, and I had the brilliant idea of heading to Idaho Falls to the nearest shopping mecca in the state, killing two birds (or ewes, in this instance) with one stone by taking our freshly judged, award-winning sheep to slaughter in nearby Driggs on the way. Obviously, we had to wear our best mid-90s attire for such an adventure, because you never knew when you might bump into a hot, chiseled, Mormon, Idaho farmer boy, be it at the slaughterhouse or the mall. I wore a very trendy, oversized white t-shirt with a side pull (you hot chicks from the 90s remember), white shorts, and white tennies. We cruised downtown Jackson with our windows rolled down, sheep bleating in anxiety and Tom Petty blasting from the speakers.

Suddenly my sister, then 17, slammed on the brakes for a tourist who was more interested in gawking than watching the signal. Tires screeched. Girls screamed. Sheep went flying. We were in the middle of the intersection with every single creature in the car in the front seat: four teenage girls and three sheep. I found myself wedged against the dash with two fattened ewes.

During the summer months, Jackson Hole swells from 6,000 to over 1,000,000 visitors thanks to tourism. Horns were honking, people were yelling, and cameras were flashing. Someone opened the door to our mustard yellow chariot, spilling out blonde hair and white wool. Now when sheep get nervous, they excrete their anxieties from pretty much every orifice. My outfit had suddenly changed color from Tide white to excrement brown and urine yellow. Yes, we had the bodily fluids of grand champion sheep dripping everywhere.

My dad raised me right, so of course I had a sharp pocket knife to rescue the screeching sheep's hoof from my hair, leaving some unintentional layers in my sweet 90s coif. What then transpired was something out of National Lampoon, with sheep running loose, girls lying in the middle of the intersection, helpless with laughter, and, by this time, cops surrounding the car.

The tourists got to see a little bit of real Jackson Hole that day. We were famous as the sheep-shit girls. Many years later, when I need something to get me through, I think of these innocent memories of simple, joyous times and I revel that once I was a sheep-shit girl. I guess I still am.

CHAPTER TWO:

Trouble in Paradise

In the thawing spring of my thirteenth year, I had no idea that my world was about to melt down around me. During those months, I had travelled to China and Japan with my grandparents on a four-week exploration of the ancient ways of Asia. It was an incredible time, but honestly, all I could think of was getting back home to the ranch, seeing the horses get kicked back out to their summer pastures, and smelling the rich, dark dirt unearthed from under the heavy snow of the previous seven months.

I loved the whoops and calls of the lanky sand hill cranes as they returned to their marshy nest behind the house and brought with them the sounds of spring and hope, of fresh starts and excitement for the summer season to come. But this year had been different. One evening, just before leaving on our trip to China, I had overheard my mother and father in a heated argument. The conversation was heart wrenching, life-changing, and altogether the worst words I'd ever heard.

My father was screaming that we were losing the ranch while my mother was trying to console him with positive thoughts and prayers. I didn't want to believe these words. I wanted to erase them from my consciousness. I prayed and I prayed hard: "Heavenly Father, please don't let us lose the ranch. I believe in you and know that you are in charge and that we must have faith."

I recited this prayer for months. I was good at it, as I'd been taught from a very young age to pray. You can always tell a Mormon prayer because it begins with, "Our dear, kind, Heavenly Father," and ends with, "I say these things in the name of Jesus Christ, amen." In the Church of Latter Day Saints (LDS), faith and prayer are imprinted upon its youth as repetitiously as halter-breaking a young colt. Our days started with prayer and scriptures and ended with prayers and scriptures, and there were prayers at every meal or event. As a result, I was highly familiar with and reliant upon prayer.

But that spring, my prayers weren't answered. While my grandparents and I were in China, a vicious and litigious battle began on the home front. At the time, my father had two partners in Heart Six Ranch, both wealthy hunters he'd been guiding for 15 years. As the partner with working interest, my dad took the ranch from a run-down, mouse-infested, ramshackle property to one of the most thriving dude ranches of its time. But land prices were starting to skyrocket in Jackson, and his partners saw it as a good time to sell. Dad, of course, wanted to keep running the business as usual. The ranch had been his dream.

So it began: the fighting, the lawyers, the lying, the deceptions, and the heartache. We were losing the ranch, and it was a dark time. My father was deeply angry and murmured the words of a crazy man. He became dark and unpredictable, saying he would hurt these men or hurt himself—and I believed he would do it. Never had I been so scared.

My perfect dream of a life was starting to crumble. I couldn't pray hard enough. Why weren't my prayers working? Was I not faithful enough? Did I not read the scriptures enough? Maybe it was because I was cussing. I stopped cussing, but it didn't help. By the middle of the summer, my entire family, all the way down to my three-year-old brother, had a restraining order against us barring us from what we had known as our own property, right across the street from our house. We were no longer allowed to step foot onto the ranch, and it had gone into receivership.

I spent days watching out my window as people I had never seen before rode my horse, my beautiful Tinker-bell, no longer mine and now just another in a string of dude horses. This broke me. My spark of kindness and humanity waned, and I could feel my heart harden. I have a vivid, visceral memory of the day when we were served papers from the sheriff telling us that we had 24 hours to get our belongings off the ranch. My dad was not allowed on the property at all, even to claim what was his. So my mom, Vanessa, and I, along with some dear friends, loaded up the horse trailers as fast as we could with odd and ends that we thought were ours. Truly, we didn't know what to take and what to leave.

I didn't know, at that age, that all these things were beyond my control. I thought, "I guess this is what happens when you pray hard for something. Maybe prayers work opposite?" I didn't doubt myself—I had been as faithful and prayerful and religious as ever—so I concluded that somehow, my religion had it backwards. Maybe you are supposed to pray for the reverse of the outcome you want? Because that is what I got.

From that moment on, I started putting intention behind the opposite of what I wanted from my prayer. If I wanted to pass a test, I would pray to fail. If I wanted to place as grand champion at the fair, I would see myself losing. This, too, worked—sometimes. Now I was just completely confused. This ritual of prayer that I had come to rely on so heavily in my life was leaving me more desperate than ever.

It was hard, but I learned from this that prayer is more than a wish. Prayer is the practice of support we seek from our higher selves, the divine, and God. Prayer doesn't give us what we want, but in fact invites action, showing us graciously the divine awakening of what our souls need in order to transform into our greater selves. A wish is just that, a wish. It cannot be acted upon; it is singular and one-sided. A prayer is a question, a plea that creates space for something to happen, and whoever you pray to creates relationship. This opens the door for our perspectives to widen and our hearts to open for change.

But I didn't know this all back then. My life as I knew it was spiraling out of control. We still had the theatre and continued to work it. But the depression and rage vibrating from my father left violence, neglect, and pure chaos in its wake. Nothing was the same. My father hardly ever smiled, and most of his communications took the form of infuriated fits. My mother withdrew emotionally, silently going through the motions of what it took to keep six kids (my youngest two siblings weren't born yet) dressed and fed.

Times were very rough. My father went to California for a while to clear his head, regroup, and figure out what he was doing with his life. It was a positive thing for him, but to me it felt like betrayal, and this, too, broke my spirit. How could he leave us when I needed him most? I would go grocery shopping with Mom, and we'd get to the check-out counter and find her credit card had been declined. We'd leave as she wept, wondering how she was going to feed her kids.

My siblings and I were left to fend for each other and ourselves. If we needed a hug, we went to each other. If we needed to talk, we went to each other. If we needed love, we went to each other. If we got into a fight at school with a classmate, we took matters into our own hands and stood up for each other. We no longer looked to our parents for such things, mostly because we didn't want to upset them any more than they already were, but also, I think, because instinctively we knew they couldn't provide what we were seeking. We kept going. Kept doing. Just like you do when life happens. You're in survival mode, and there's only space for basic needs to get met. Nothing cushy. Nothing great. We were focused on just making it from day to day.

Rites of Passage

That summer, we moved above the theatre to get away from having to look across the street at the ranch we used to own. My mom hired me as an ensemble cast member in our production of Oklahoma. With all that was going on around me, this was a dream come true. Here was my chance to be taken seriously and grow as a performer. The cast was filled with beautiful people— actors, dancers, and singers. I met some of my dearest friends that summer. A summer of passage, if you will.

Unfortunately, it was also a passage I wasn't ready for in other ways. There was a young man in the show in his early twenties with whom I became quite smitten. He had wavy, blond hair, smoky, blue-hazel eyes, tantalizing sex appeal, and a badass car. I would be 14 that September, but I looked more like 18, with big, tight breasts, strong dancing legs, and my own luscious, blonde locks.

I was just starting to get noticed by men—the way you don't want to get noticed. Like when your dad's friend sees you in your swimsuit and says, "Wow, you've really grown into a woman," or the high school boys come to watch track meets to see your tits bounce and yell at you as you round the last quarter-mile, or when all the boys call you "dick tease" because you want to be friends but you don't want to have a boyfriend. Yeah, that kind of notice.

26

This new guy at the theatre had been giving me a lot of attention, especially in private when it was just the two of us: butt pinching, boob grazing, little whispers. It was really overwhelming for me, and I didn't know how to deal with it. I had never thought of myself as desirable—my older sister was the pretty one, and I was the funny one. Also, having been raised Mormon, where even sexual thoughts were shunned, the idea of having any fantasies come to fruition with a guy ten years older than me was out of the question. Over the course of several weeks, our private meetings turned more and more heated. We hid backstage in the dark wings, making out heavily during the show while the other cast members were on stage.

It didn't help that times were so hard at home in our apartment above the theatre. My dad was a depressed, rageful disaster. My mom was very distracted trying to keep the kids wrangled and fed, not to mention keeping a tight watch on Dad so he didn't do something crazy. My older sister and I had massive responsibilities that summer. In addition to working nightly at the theatre, we were driving back and forth the 40 miles to and from the old house in Moran, where we still had to feed our 4-H animals. I felt alone and rebellious, as well as scared, frustrated, and angry, but all those hard emotions seemed to slip away when I had the attention of this man. I felt like I mattered. I felt safe. And I was curious and excited—until, that is, I realized that he didn't acknowledge my presence when we were around others.

Suddenly, I didn't feel so special. In fact I felt bad,

but that didn't stop me from going back for more—more secret gatherings, more slight kisses in passing. We grew bolder. Almost every night, I'd sneak out the window of our upstairs apartment, shimmy down the back ladder, cross the dark, dirty alley, and cautiously creak open the loud, ragged door that led into the dilapidated blue house where all the boys in the summer show were living. I would then kneel at the bedroom door, heart racing, trying to convince myself to leave and then talking myself into staying. Finally, I would push the door open, crawl over to his bed, and slide into the cool sheets where I knew he was waiting.

We'd kiss, his hot, smoky, cigarette breath on my lips and his hands slipping into my "sexy" panties from Kmart, touching me in ways that left me begging for more and also deeply ashamed. After several hours of this, I'd have scratches on my cheeks from his rough, unshaven skin, proof of our sordid affair I'd carry the next day. As dawn began to melt away the condensation on the one dirty window in the place, I'd begin my mixed emotive journey home. Past lonely boys sleeping, past other couples entangled in a summer romance, out the obnoxiously loud door into the crisp morning air. I'd jog down the trash-laden dirt alley, climb up the steep ladder back into the window on the roof, and rush back to bed before my family woke up. Before the screaming of the kids, and the screaming of Dad. Before day really began, I'd rest for a couple more hours, sleeping away the feeling of abuse and dirtiness, pretending it was a dream and knowing that it was wrong. I'm sure everyone knew what we were doing—or, rather, what he was doing—but no one ever tried to stop him. I didn't either.

He didn't acknowledge my existence unless I was lying in his bed with my panties down. If we were around others, I was a ghost, a hushed secret. I wore his curse of shame and guilt heavy around my middle for years: don't look at me, I am filth and shame rolled into a vulnerable ball of 13-year-old flesh, unworthy of true love.

While I was writing this book, I sent a copy of this chapter to the high school boyfriend I later took up with. I wanted to share what I had brought to our teenage relationship back then. I hadn't been able to trust his love because of what happened with this older guy. I was unable to be loved because I had seen so much deception and damage.

After he read my story, he replied aloofly, "Oh, I thought you were, like, really raped." Those invalidating words reeled me back 20 years. I was stripped naked all over again, once again a 13-year-old girl with shame, guilt, and invalidation smeared across my pain.

Given his reaction, I'm glad I didn't also share with him what had happened later that same confusing summer. My family had taken our 4-H animals to show at the county fair in Jackson. Usually this was my favorite time of year, but that summer, with so much change and pain going on, I was numb to the joy that I usually received from showing and the tasks that went along with it. I was very dutiful about my responsibilities. It meant a great deal to me to keep our pens clean and our area where we kept the steers looking tidy.

There had been two young men in their late teens hanging around the livestock tent quite a bit that week. Occasionally, they talked to me. They were not from Jackson, but I had assumed they were friends with some of our other fellow 4-H-ers even though I had never seen them interacting with anyone. One of them was a big guy—cute enough—and the other, ever so slightly smaller, came across like a timid tag along. They looked old enough to be seniors in high school, maybe even high school graduates.

The more charismatic one asked me if I would go on a date with him, but I refused. He asked me several different times over a couple days to go to the carnival with him, get an ice cream, or go out to dinner. I wasn't interested. I look back now and wonder if my shutting him down is what triggered him.

I had gone to the carnival late one night with a group of other friends who lived in Moran. It was a long drive, and they had to hurry to get home before their curfew. They asked me if I needed a ride back to the theatre, but I'd forgotten to feed the steers at the fair, so I decided to do so and then walk the couple of blocks home. We said our goodbyes near the parking area behind the carnival.

I walked alone back to the livestock tent. I figured I'd not only feed the steers, but also do a little cleanup around the pens so I could sleep in a little in the morning. The livestock tent was well-lit, with lots of 4-H folk sleeping in their live-in horse trailers or campers and parked only a few feet away, so I never even questioned doing any of this alone. Besides, Jackson Hole was one of the safest places in the world—everyone knew that no one locked their cars or houses.

As I was raking hay, I heard a voice behind me. "Hey what are you doing here?"

I turned around. There were the two guys I had seen hanging around the last couple days. Naively, I went about my chores, saying I needed to get it all done before I went to bed. They heckled me a little, teasing that I should just go home with them. Laughing it off, I told them I had a show in the morning. In case it might make them back off, I even told them I was Mormon.

It didn't work. The charismatic guy's tone turned darker and deeper. He got in really close behind me, grabbed the rake, and said, "You're really pretty, ya know," as the other one snickered behind him.

I grabbed the rake back. I was getting nervous. All of a sudden, I questioned every choice I had made that night. Why had I come over alone? Why hadn't I just gotten a ride home with my friends? Why did I even care about raking the stupid steer pen? I had been in fist fights before and had my ass handed to me by big horses and steers. I knew I was tough, but I didn't want to have to find out how tough. I backed away slowly, saying, "I have to get home. My parents are waiting on me."

Both guys moved in closer, cornering me, coercing me, telling me to just come with them. Were they drunk? On drugs? I had no idea what was going down, I just kept looking around for the quickest route of escape. I figured I'd hit the big one with the rake, jump over the steers, climb as fast as I could over the fence, and then run like

31

hell. I was a really fast runner, and the second guy was chubby and out of shape.

Backing up, I slammed the rake into the bigger guy's head, snapping the implement in two. I turned and jumped up the fence, then felt him grab my leg and pull me down. Screaming, I felt a huge blow to the left side of my face. Blood gushed from my nose as my eye swelled shut. Then came a sensation I knew all too well—NOOOOO, I was going to pass out! I fought like hell, blindly punching, hitting, scratching, and trying to scream. I took another punch to the left side of my face. The effects from the blow were almost immediate, and the seconds of fighting that ensued felt like an eternity.

What followed was a horrific scene I've never spoken of in detail until now. In and out of consciousness, I was barely able to track what was happening. I only remember flashes of what came next: them dragging me and holding me down, the smell of beer, my face being slammed into the hay stack. I was kicking and trying to scream but no sound came out—someone had their hand over my mouth. I couldn't see what was going on. My hands and legs were being held down. Someone pulled my hair back. With that, it became too painful to hold onto consciousness. I tried to let go and pass out. I went limp.

When I regained consciousness, I was face down over a hay stack. I immediately flashed to what had happened and jumped up, screaming and fighting, then fell down hard onto the dirty rutted road. I realized that my pants were down around my ankles. I was dizzy and crying. I hurt everywhere. Scanning my body, I realized my nose was bloody and sore to the touch, that my neck hurt like hell, and that it felt like I'd battled for days. With horror, I noticed a trickle of blood dripping down the inside of my right thigh.

I was alone amidst the scattered trash and loose hay, an arm's length away from the huge metal bin that held all the used wood shavings full of horse and cow shit from the pens. Just feet away was the well-lit livestock tent full of grand champion steers, lambs, and pigs. Beyond that were the horse trailers and campers full of my friends and other 4-H-ers resting for the big day tomorrow. It seemed impossible that no one had heard anything or even come out to check.

I pulled my pants back up, exhausted, crying, and trying to figure a way to wear my ripped t-shirt so that it covered my breasts. I ended up turning it around and letting the ripped front hang down my back. I had never felt so alone. It was late, and, sobbing, I staggered my way back to the theatre where my parents were sleeping.

Then panic set in. What was I going to tell them? Dad would for sure kill anyone in his path to find these guys, and then he'd be in jail for sure. No, I couldn't have that. He was already on the verge of a breakdown. They hadn't wanted me to go out late that night, so this was all my fault.

Wait, I worried. Were those guys still there? Would they follow me? I started running from dark corner to dark corner, avoiding the streetlights. The night was eerily calm, and I didn't pass a single soul. I wanted to get home as fast as possible, but I was also terrified of what I would say when I got there. My face was throbbing, my crotch was aflame, and my legs were shaking. I passed by the rickety blue house where my other shameful sexual encounter had taken place—it was too much to take in. I just needed to get home.

I was barely able to lift my legs up the steep steps into the apartment. Hurriedly, I got into the shower and vigorously scrubbed away any proof of what might have happened, soaping every nook and every crease, violently scrubbing even my vagina as hard as I could. Although it hurt so bad I wanted to scream, I also wanted every shred of evidence off my body. I was disgusted with myself. How could I have let this happen? How come I wasn't stronger? Why wasn't I tougher? I just wanted to sleep, maybe forever. I slipped out of the shower and, putting on my baggiest sweat pants and t-shirt, went and lay on the floor next to my parents' bed on Dad's side. I pulled his hand out from under the covers, held it tight, and silently cried.

"Honey-girl, what's the matter?" Dad whispered.

I wanted to tell him, but I was so terrified, so ashamed. "Nothing, Dad, I had a bad dream."

"Okay, try to get some rest. Big day tomorrow."

"Can I sleep right here?" I asked.

But he was already back to slumbering peacefully. I lay there on the floor, shaking and shivering and hanging onto his hand like it was the only hope I had left in the world.

The next morning was a bustle and hustle to get back to the fairgrounds. I awoke hoping that the night before had been a dream, but every inch of my body said otherwise. I was sore like I'd been riding a bucking horse for a week. Mom asked what had happened to my face, and without missing a beat, I said, "Rachael's steer kicked me last night when I was feeding him."

"Wow Jess, that's bad. You're going to look horrible for the show today."

"Yeah," I said meekly.

Then it was on to business as usual, with everyone getting dressed, all the siblings asking what happened, gathering the outfits for show, and hurrying, as we didn't want to be late. And as fast as the whole ordeal had happened, I tucked it away into the deep, dark parts of my mind where no one could see it our touch it. Especially me.

But from then on, when someone would grab my neck weirdly, I would have a flash of memories. When my boyfriend tried to go too far, I would panic, cry, and then retreat emotionally from him for weeks. Or if there were a rape scene or a woman getting beaten in a movie, I would need to leave immediately. These were the only hints left that any abuse had ever happened to me, and that's how I wanted it. I never let myself get too close to any men after that, ever. It took years into my marriage before I was able to really accept my husband's love and trust.

I didn't really want to include this bit of my story because it still carries so much weight for me. And in the first draft of this book, I didn't. I hadn't wanted to put any more energy into what took so many years to undo. I also

35

was afraid of being rejected by you who are reading this now. I thought you might think this was too much. You might stop reading right here. You might not believe me. And then I would hide, reeling back into my deep, dark corner of shame and guilt.

I was afraid to share this with my family. I didn't want them to know. I didn't even want my husband to know all the sordid details. But I've come to understand that I cannot edit and chop myself up, telling only bits and pieces of my story and leaving me shattered into pieces. I am who I am today because of all of it, the dark and the light. "Only in the darkness," it is said, "can you see the stars."

So please see me: this is my darkness. But I also have shards of beautiful light breaking through, tiny specks of brilliance scattered and waiting for the dawn.

In later years, I came to know that every single one of my best friends had been victim to some sort of early sexual encounter and/or abuse. Since Jackson Hole is a tourist town, there are a large number of young transients who come to work seasonally. Each of my friends was swayed into a secret relationship with a man older than they by at least 10 years. How does this happen? I am dumbfounded by the fact that 90 percent of the women in my life have been sexually abused. That means nine out of 10 of my friends! Absolutely terrifying.

Now that my friends and I are mothers, we do what we can to lead our children to honor and hold themselves and others with the utmost respect. We teach our daughters to be strong and to understand the value of the gifts they hold. If being a mother is not for you, know that we need your voice also in the workplace, in art, all of our voices ringing loud and people standing together hand in hand against the misogynistic past, uniting in our quest for balance of the feminine and masculine energies. For there cannot be one without the other.

CHAPTER THREE:

Becoming

It's no wonder I struggled with the morality of sexual attraction. The Mormon church connects sex before marriage to shame, and it's overwhelming. Not once was I taught to embrace my sexuality. Instead, women were shamed into modesty and covering up. Don't you dare arouse the boys! I didn't seem to have a lot of control over that.

My parents hadn't believed in the school system teaching us about sex, so I was always escorted out of the room to another activity when sex ed was the topic. The problem was, no one else taught me either. I got my first period while away at a swim meet. I was an avid swimmer and usually placed first in all my events, but the day before that particular meet I was feeling incredibly tired, like my arms were weighed down by concrete. At practice before the competition, I noticed a dull, mysterious aching in my lower back.

That evening after practice, my girlfriends and I walked to the nearest pizza joint. I had on a cute white tee and white denim shorts I adored with tiny sunflowers printed on the back. I was ravenously hungry and I ate more food than I can ever remember eating at one time. Then I grabbed my to-go bag of Reese's peanut butter cups, because I wanted chocolate, now. As I stood up from the table in the middle of the restaurant, I saw that my bright, white denim shorts were stained a deep, dark red. Had I dropped pizza in my lap and didn't remember? I tried wiping the mess up with napkin, and my girlfriends and I laughed on the way home about my clumsiness.

I was in the bathroom changing into my pjs when I realized my underwear was soaked in red too. What was it? Was it blood? Blood! I screamed, having no idea what it all meant. I had heard of periods, but I was totally uninformed about of all the signs of its impending onset. My swim coach (who happened to be my best friend's mom) came running to the door and, once she saw what was going on, explained everything to me. Words like "blossom blooming" and "becoming" were all that stayed with me. I was appalled and felt robbed of my youth and innocence. I didn't want this. I wasn't ready. How was I going to swim?

She gave me a box of maximum absorbance tampons, told me to read the back and follow the directions, and then left as quickly as she'd come in. So between the tears and the terror, I followed the directions, put a leg up on the toilet, and, after several failed attempts, slid the oversized cotton plug inside.

I felt like I couldn't walk. It felt like there was an iron sledge hammer wedged between my hip bones. There is no way that this was how it was supposed to feel! But with no other reference point, I simply hobbled to bed to cry and wish my mom were there to hold me. I didn't sleep much that night.

The next morning, I put on my best attitude. I put my tampon in, swimsuit on, and sweatpants low on my hips so there was nothing touching my cramping stomach and aching back. As we drove to the pool, my teammates kept pestering me, wondering what was wrong and why I wasn't "fun" like usual. I just wanted to hide the fact that I was bleeding—and that I had that weird tail thing hanging out of my body.

I lost every race that day, and I had never lost one before. I couldn't stop crying, and I had never cried in front of people. At our house, crying got you nowhere. I couldn't believe that this was what it meant to become a woman, or that no one had told me what was in store. I wanted to rewind the clock and go back to simpler times without breasts, hormones, periods, and sordid sexual desires. When we were just wild fairy children racing our ponies through the woods without a care in the world. The walls of my fairyland were shaking down around me. The heavy lifting of being a woman was just beginning.

*Horse: The **horse** is a universal symbol of freedom without restraint, because riding a **horse** makes people feel they can free themselves from their own bindings.*

Our life was starting to find a new rhythm. My dad had calmed down a little from the deep effects of losing

Heart Six Ranch, and he was on a mission to rebuild. He spent the next couple of years looking around Wyoming for the next best fit for us, a place to rebuild his dream, his values, and his sense of self-worth after losing everything.

Finally, we came across the Triangle C Ranch 35 minutes east of our Buffalo Valley home. It was in the opposite direction from Jackson and the theatre, but it was perfect. It needed a lot of work and love, but who better to see its potential than Dad? He had a way of seeing things not as they were, but as they could be. He was charismatic and vibrant enough to make others believe it too, then push them to a place to get it done as he wanted.

I spent most of my seasons at the new ranch now and less time at the theatre. I was seeking solace and respite after my bad sexual experience and the consequences of the abuse. I was lashing out at high school and dabbling in smoking weed and drinking. Neither of those things felt good to me, but I was trying to forget, to get my mind away from sexual abuse, deception, betrayal, shame, and also the pain of losing our first ranch. I was not privy to awakenings at this young age, but I could sense that I was on the edge of one. Awakenings, as I have come to define them, mean coming into one's own existence or awareness. I was soon to become aware of myself in an entirely new way.

As always, I found forgiveness, strength, and rehabilitation on horseback, and took solace in being out in the wilderness, the fresh mountain air whisking away all my cares amidst the vastness of nature, solitude, and silence. I was slowly healing. I could be myself again—the singing, dancing, dreaming cowgirl I knew I was.

It was the summer before my junior year. My sister, who I considered my best friend, had just graduated and was off to her own life, and I was left at home to finally spread my wings a little now that I would not be in her shadow. The new ranch was my haven.

This was also a pivotal year for me, in that I realized that life with alcohol and drugs wasn't a path I wanted to continue down. I didn't feel at my peak or connected to my higher self when doing these things.

Alcohol had played an interesting role in my life. As a Mormon, I had never been around drinking culture growing up. We were not allowed to drink. My parents didn't drink. My grandparents didn't drink. I experimented, like most teenagers, but drinking never felt good to me. Intuitively, my body didn't like it and rejected it. I would drink small amounts and have incredible reactions and massive hangovers even after consuming so little. I had also noticed that I tended to experiment with drinking during the very painful times of my life, when I couldn't deal with the weight of my reality. I wish I would have seen then that being sober was a gift and one of the greatest morals of the Mormon church, but I was rebelling against the church, against everything I had been taught, and I was seeking my own path.

I didn't know how to not be Mormon besides drinking. At that time, that, to me, was the only real difference. So I dabbled with alcohol and promiscuity, seeking to mask the parts of me that I couldn't bear to look at. I wanted enlightenment and freedom. I knew horses, music, and nature gave me that, but I wanted to find those experiences. At the ranch, where I was mostly removed from any social life or pressures, I found I didn't need the veil of substances to feel good.

This was our first summer at the Triangle C Ranch in Dubois, Wyoming. I was so happy to be back on a ranch shoveling shit, feeding horses, wrangling them in from pasture in the breaking twilight, and keeping them fresh. I loved it when our horses got a little "broncy," which is another way to say spirited and rowdy. I had fun riding bucking horses through the freshly dewed willows, skimming the river, over and undering 'em, and crow hopping (a style of bucking where the horse arches its back and takes short, stiff hops) all the way back to the corral.

My father had left me in charge of six guests. I was supposed to guide them to our new camp, a three-hour horseback ride into the Shoshone National Forest and the densest population of grizzlies in the lower 48, and to a place called the Dunoir (one of my most sacred places on Earth). I was to saddle the horses, load them up in the trailer, and drive the equines and their enthusiasts for an hour up a long dirt road to the trailhead. On arrival, I was supposed to unload horses, get the humans on them, and start the journey to the camp I knew only from the map my father had drawn on a napkin at breakfast the day before.

So there I was, 14 years old, my blonde hair bopping

behind the wheel of the one-ton crew cab Ford busting at the sides with six folks who were likely praying for their lives and wondering what in the hell they had gotten themselves into. I was nervous, but I also knew I was prepared. In fact, I probably had more experience in the backcountry than all of these adults combined.

I unloaded the horses and realized that one of the women was probably not going to be able to get on her horse by herself. She was older, stout, and had been blessed with short legs—none of which added up to a good recipe for trying to get on a horse in the woods if you weren't experienced. Usually a stump or downed log would work well in this situation, but the trailhead had recently been cleaned up, so I was going to have to resort to a steep ledge and sheer willpower to get this woman on her horse.

We all eyed each other: me in my teenage glory, her feeling vulnerable, and the fine steed, who was looking back at us with the look of, "Ah, hell NO, you isn't!" I gently instructed the nice woman to raise her leg to the stirrup so I could place my shoulder up under her ass and shove her up onto old Big Mac, a proud Appaloosa. On a count of three, we gave it our all—to no avail. I reassured her to not worry, and we got at it again: One, two, three! And with a final heave-ho, she swung her leg up halfway, kicking poor Big Mac in the rump.

Big Mac lunged forward. I jumped with him, positioning both my hands on each fleshy cheek of the woman to catch her from a nasty fall, and gave her a shove with all my might. She gave all her might too. With my face

45

perfectly placed between her two voluptuous buns, she burst forth a wave of flatulence with such force that it spooked me and the horse and echoed off the face of the nearby peaks. I laughed so hard that my already trembling arms went limp, and I fell, rolling backwards, down the steep slope just like Wesley in The Princess Bride. "As YOUUUUUU wish!" Finally, I came to a sliding stop and stood, picking the nest of twigs and pine needles from my hair. My unattended guests shouted from above, "You okay?"

"Yep," I laughed back as I made the trek up the hill. I hopped on my horse and led the group down the trail and into the dark forest. We got lost for about an hour, but I was the only one who really knew. The smiles and belly laughs had turned a nervous ride into a relaxed, happy one.

Laughter has saved me in many of awkward situations. I'm very grateful that I've had the gumption to laugh when I felt it. My laughter is one of my most powerful tools. It sometimes comes to me in waves so hard and strong that it leaves me weak and breathless, then recedes with a gentle smile. Laughter transitions the world from dark to light.

Most of my days were spent guiding guests on the trails. Horses are an extension of my spirit, a true reflection of my inner being. Underneath all the layers of abuse, discouragement, violence, and disappointment was a naïve, spirited little girl wanting so deeply to move beyond the circumstances that had thus far shaped her. I was a laughing, light human looking to soar. I used to imagine myself as a wild horse, running and soaring over a desert floor, the sweet smell of broken sage filling my flared nostrils with each deep breath and a swift breeze catching my mane and tail at every leap.

In this vision, my gait is strong and beautiful, and I am free and fast. I'm bounding and leaping across rocks, plunging into rivers, and paddling calmly with my head barely above the water. I've never been touched by man. In fact, I've only seen glimpses of him from afar as I stampede past like lightning. No ropes of guilt, shame, or fear bind me, and the only hurt I know is that of harsh winters and dry summers. I dream of peaceful nights among the moonlit plains, the days spent nose-down and belly-deep in the sweet grass.

Into the Fall

I went back to school at the Jackson Hole High school that junior year as a non-partyer. It shocked many members of the beer-drinking crowd. "Wow, Jess, you used to be so wild (their meaning of wild and mine were completely opposite). What happened?" That year was one of the best years of my life, and I'm grateful to have experienced its clarity and forgiveness. As I look back, it seems that my intuition and my spirit were urging me to enjoy and to live as fully as I could, for I would need my strength for what was to come.

I spent most of that year digging deep into music, drama, and my 4-H projects. Things had been running fairly smoothly at home and at the ranch. I would go to school during the week, then head to the ranch to help work it on the weekend. Time flew, as we were so busy. My mother gave birth to my youngest sibling Cheyenne in April of that year. There was much going on with eight kids (my sister now gone to college) and two businesses. My parents relied on me heavily to jump in at times when they could not, whether it be at the ranch, the theatre, or helping at home.

That spring, I auditioned for The Sound of Music at school, and was given the lead part of Maria. That was a huge affirmation for me that I was on the right path in pursuing my dream of singing and entertaining. Many of my best friends were cast in that show also. We spent the nights rehearsing, laughing, and becoming closer than ever before.

Being part of a theatre family is something I wish the whole world could experience. You take a random group of people, throw them into a very vulnerable situation (like singing, dancing, and acting in front of huge crowds), and they end up being best friends (or worst enemies) for life.

In a strange way, it reminds me of being out in the woods with others: you have to rely on the wit, grit, and creativity of those around you. In the theatre, you step on stage, trusting that the other person knows their stuff as well as you, and that if you mess up, they can catch you. It is exactly the same as going into the wilderness, where you need those others to be wise enough to know their way and what to do in case of an emergency.

It's not just theatre and wilderness survival: it's life. Have you ever been cast in a role that you can study and thrive in? Are you prepared and knowledgeable in case of an emergency, like those around you forgetting their lines, or a grizzly attack? Did you choose the right cast to carry and enhance your role? Are you prepared to spend a night with no food, shelter, or water? How do you react in dire situations? Do you run offstage, embarrassed because you forgot your line, or do you own it, laugh at yourself, and move on? It is all relative, my friends. In the small aspects of you is how you do your big life.

CHAPTER FOUR:

Leap of Faith

In October of 1997, I had barely turned 17 and was crushing my senior year of high school. Life was so good. I had spent my summer at our family ranch, taking trail rides, seeking the deepest skinny-dipping holes of the Wind River, and perfecting my s'more-roasting skills. As winter approached, I was getting ready to graduate the following spring, and was excited for my future. Both at our family theatre and at school, I was being prepped for a career in musical theatre. I had my sights set on The Cincinnati Conservatory of Music, and my choir teacher was really pulling for me to go there.

We were in the midst of setting up my audition and visit to Cincinnati. For the preceding week, I'd had this daunting feeling that something was wrong. I couldn't explain it. I felt a strong, underlying anxiety. One day, my mom had found me sitting in my closet and crying.

"What's wrong, Jess?"

"I think I need to go to the doctor and get checked out," I'd cried. "Something doesn't feel right in me."

"You're okay, honey," she'd said. "There is a lot going on in life, this will pass."

I had deeply wanted to feel this reassurance, but I hadn't. The nagging, dull sensation had continued to tug at my spirit. On the evening of October 29, we had our fall choir concert. We were performing at Walk Festival Hall in Teton Village. It was a huge venue, and we were tasked with taking down the risers and chairs and cleaning up after the evening's events. I was there until late in the night.

The next morning, October 30, I woke up late for school and had to rush to get to my first class, which was weightlifting. Everything seemed off that day. I got to the locker room to change and found that my locker had been broken into and my clothes stolen. I had to borrow a friend's shorts and t-shirt for the day.

It was a big day: the day we were to satisfy the physical fitness requirement of running the obstacle course. The course consisted of a suicide run, a rope climb, scaling a wall up to the second- story level where we were to army crawl under chairs, jump to the gym floor from second level, and then scale a rope wall. I'm sure I'm forgetting a few of the obstacles. I didn't pay close attention. I didn't know that what was soon to transpire would change me forever.

I still had the uneasy, edgy feeling that something was wrong with me. I approached my teacher and asked her if there was any way I could complete the course another day. "No," she said. "We're taking it down tomorrow, sorry."

I had strong reservations and did not feel comfortable doing the course that day. But you had to do the course in order to receive a grade—or flunk the semester, which would mean I wouldn't graduate.

The course was timed, and the faster you completed it, the better your grade. We were asked to line up against the wall and to start the course in intervals. As the first few kids began, I asked my friend behind me in line to save my spot. Quickly, I ran to the locker room, dropped to my knees, and said the most heartfelt, earnest prayer of my existence.

"Heavenly Father, please be with me today. I don't know what is wrong. I don't know what is going to happen. I'm scared. Please help me be brave for whatever is coming. I need your guidance, support, and love. Thank you, Heavenly Father. Amen."

I jogged back out to my place in line and found that it was my turn to begin. I have never been the kind of person to do anything half-assed, so I went full-out to try my hardest. I started strong, ran strong, and felt strong. I pulled myself hand over hand up the long rope and ran to scale the wall. I army crawled as fast as my elbows would take me. I was nailing it!

Then I got to the jump. I hopped the rail, just as I had the day before in practice. As I soared out, 23 feet above the gym floor, I suddenly realized the mat was not below me. The mat was not below me!

Where was it? I was in mid-air with literally no safety

net. I panicked and tried to back-pedal, flailing my arms and legs in a futile attempt to hurl my body backwards.

Contact. My feet hit first. My legs crumpled, and my face slammed into my knees. I heard screaming, yelling. "Is she okay?" "What happened?"

I couldn't see. There was too much blood in my eyes. I tried getting up, and lightning bolts of pain shot up my legs. My legs couldn't support me. I tried again. Why could I not stand? Again, there was no response from my legs.

Someone came to my side. I couldn't tell who it was. The blood from my nose was everywhere. "Jessica, can you hear me?"

"Yes," I managed to reply relatively calmly. Shock was starting to set in.

"Where does it hurt?"

Fucking everywhere. "My legs," I said from a distance.

There was a flurry of shouting. "Her nose, hurry, get ice, get something, go get the nurse!"

"My legs, my legs hurt," I tried to tell them. I knew from previous injuries that I had broken my nose, and I was familiar with the stinging eyes and numb cheeks. But I had never felt such excruciating pain in my legs. "Please, my legs."

"Okay," someone said, "take her shoes off." At this point there were several people around me, some of whom I could recognize by the sound of their voices. My eyes were hurting and blurry. With a tug that seemed as though I was getting beaten by a baseball bat, my shoes were removed.

I felt the sudden, shocking sensation of my feet falling off. That couldn't be right. I couldn't fathom it. "They're falling," I murmured. "Help me, please."

I was still oddly calm. Somehow, amidst the pain, my prayer had been answered: "Help me be brave for whatever is coming."

I heard someone say, "I think they're sprained. Let's call her parents. Jessica, where are your parents?"

"I don't know," I answered. "Try home. Try the ranch, the theatre."

After what seemed like an eternity, I finally heard hope: the sound of someone talking to my mother on the phone. "Vicki, Jess has been in an accident at the school. Looks like she has broken her nose and sprained her ankles. Would you like us to take her to the hospital?... Yes, she's right here, would you like to speak to her?"

"Jess?" My mother's voice brought incredible warmth, hope, and reassurance. I could be strong, but I needed her. "Jess, are you hurt?'

"Yes, Mom, it's bad."

"Do you need to go to the hospital?"

"Yes, Mom, hurry." My ability to keep it together was waning.

After the school officials spoke to my mother and asked me, like I had any clarity, what they should do, there was finally a decision to take me to the hospital—not by ambulance, but in the back of the principal's station wagon. They loaded me onto a gurney, every movement like a dagger to my body, and into the car. I can remember every single pebble under the tires of that station wagon, tormenting and torturing me on the drive to the ER. Keep it together, Jess, keep focused, keep alert, I was spiritually coaching myself, whispering prayers of strength and comfort. Eight miles of shattering pain seemed like an eternity.

Busting through the doors with the gurney, we entered St. John's Medical Center, Jackson Hole's only hospital. Nurses rushed me to the examining room. I remember asking them to not cut my clothes off, as they weren't mine but had been borrowed from a friend. Without pause, they cut right up the side of my shorts, shirt, and sports bra and quickly transferred me to another gurney before rushing me to the x-ray room.

I was in so much pain it was intoxicating. There was a young man at my side asking me to move my legs in a certain way to get the x-ray. I told my leg to move in my mind, but nothing happened. I was cut off from all communication with the lower half of my body. He picked up my leg and moved it. If I'd had any strength in that moment, I would have killed him over the pain it caused me to move.

Over my own groaning and moaning, I heard the slow beep of the x-ray machine. Then came the most terrifying words I've ever heard: "Quickly, go get the doctors. This is terrible. She'll never walk again."

That was all. I blacked out from trying to stay strong and alert for the previous hour. It felt so good to just float away from consciousness. I knew, somehow, that there was rushing going on around me—doctors, nurses, my mother crying. It was as if I was there, but no longer in my pain-riddled body, like I was just floating through the ethereal vibration of what had been my past life.

I slammed back into my body just as the doctor administered morphine into my vein. My God, nothing had ever felt so good before. The drug pulsed through my veins, taking every waking pain and suffering I had ever endured along with it. No wonder people are addicted to this shit. So good. Then the haziness returned. I was present, but not awake. I was not dead, but not alive. I drifted away to an expansion unknown. I spent days there, in and out of surgeries.

The next thing, I knew, I was slowly blinking my eyes, the world swimming in and out of focus. I was trying hard to get through the concrete of the drugs that were weighing down my alertness. Then bam! I felt huge pain. I could not move my legs like usual. They felt so heavy. What was on my side? I could barely breathe.

"Jess, Jess?"

"She's awake!"

I looked over and saw my older sister holding my hand. Scanning my body, I could see large metal things sticking out from various places. Both my legs were elevated. My side was killing me—even the slightest breath brought agonizing pain. I could lift my arms, but I was so heavily sedated it took minutes for my synapses to fire.

It had been three days since the accident. I had been kept in a drug-induced coma, mostly for surgical purposes.

Then came the explanations. *Honey, your left leg is doing better, it was in 17 pieces…we were able to take some*

*bone and bone marrow from your hip to help rebuild both
ankles, but your right is not taking... It is rejecting the marrow, and we can't seem to get it to hold together... it is worse,
in 24 pieces... you've broken your nose and cheekbones, but
you just rest now.*

Oh, my God. How did I get here? What happened in
those minutes between my deep prayer and then starting
the obstacle course? Is it even possible to get this disfigured while at P.E. class at school?

I cried. I wanted to cry more, but the fog of drugs
kept me in a state in which I couldn't really feel what I
was wanting or even needing to feel. My room was a blur
of flowers, cards, candy, and get-well sentiments. I didn't
even really know what was happening. All I could make
out was that I fucking hurt. I wanted to put on a brave
face, so that is what I did. I let the tears stream silently
down the side of my crushed face, but I didn't let out the
whimpers and sobs that were building inside of me. It
was time to rest, to go back to that ethereal state of in-between. Rest now, Jess, rest.

I spent the next several days being woken every
so often to get vitals checked. The last surgery hadn't
worked, so they went in again. More drugs. A morphine drip and release at the push of my thumb. Then
all kinds of different doctors. The physical therapist.
The nurses. The people who delivered meals. The
cleaning crew. People coming to visit. Many came to
pray over me. Their prayers comforted me. I found
solace in the familiar script. *Please, God, heal this
young woman. Heal this shattered body, these broken*

bones, this broken spirit. These intentions were the thread of hope I held tightly to.

When folks visited, they must have been scared to touch any part of my body besides my hair. Every time I woke, it was to someone stroking it, which left me with extra-greasy hair. I wanted to scream, "Stop touching my hair!" but knew that would not have been well received by those who were just coming to share their love with me. What I would have done to have dry shampoo back then.

It would actually be months before I could have a proper shower, but I was able to leave the hospital after several weeks. There had been a hospital bed sent to my house to get me set up there, but let me tell you, peeps, our house was the most handicapped-unfriendly place on the planet. There were two sets of steep stairs going down just to get to the front door. Then French doors (not even close to wheelchair-width) going from the front room to the living room and from the kitchen into what we called the dance studio, which was actually our TV room. It was this room that I would call my bedroom for however long it took me to heal. At that point in time, it was looking and feeling like eternity.

When we left the hospital, my dad carried me to our van. We called it our "Vegas Van" because it had lights on the roof and on the sides. There was a back bench that converted into a bed. It was perfect for my huge family. Little did we know that it would be perfect for my new horizontal position in life. I remember being in excruciating pain when my dad lifted me. Not only did I have halos on both my legs, but I'd had hip surgery, too, so bending or moving that hip at all was absolutely breathtaking, and not in a good way.

I remember just releasing into this new constant state of pain. Resisting it was exhausting, so I would catch myself just below my pain threshold and cradle myself there. Always a little deeper than I thought I could go, and even a little longer. This became my new norm. Pain. I had to become friends with her because she was a constant visitor that had moved into my life and wasn't leaving any time soon—and maybe never. There were times when she was my only constant. Some say that time will heal all pain, but I've come to realize that time doesn't heal pain at all, but rather allows us the space to learn how to live with our pains. Time distances us from the initial blow, then separates, eludes, and even tempts us further down the path to mindfulness, the stillness where we can truly find ourselves.

One day far down the trail, I would be able to look behind me and say that this was where my life took a major detour from the life I had been expecting. It jolted me into a place I'd never been nor wanted to visit, but it was on this detour that I found my real beauty, my real strength, and who I truly am. That expected path had been simply an illusion of who I could have been. Pain brought me to who I really am. I am depth, I am grace, I am humble, I am vulnerable, I am strong, resilient, misshapen, and disfigured. I can no longer separate my pain from myself and call her it or she, because she is me.

I soon became settled in my new bedroom, with the hospital bed off to one side but in front of the TV. We didn't have television service, only movies, and we had hundreds of them. The TV room was always a bustling place with my family of 10 people. It served as the entertainment room, the mud room, and the storage room where the deep freezer sat. The only working downstairs bathroom adjoined it.

And I was stuck there. Literally, with my legs elevated above my heart, observing the bustle around me but no longer able to participate in it. Just observing. Watching my siblings get ready for school or any outdoor activity. If my siblings put on a movie I didn't want to watch, all I could do was yell and throw something that was in arm's reach at them. I would get my meals that Mom had prepared delivered to me on a hospital tray, then the rest of the family would eat their meals in the kitchen. I could hear the laughter, arguments, conversations, and mealtime prayers from a lonely distance. My accident put me in a corner: watching, but unable to participate. I still have incredible FOMO (fear of missing out) to this day.

I joke about FOMO now, but the truth is, the accident left me with an incredible drive to never miss out again on anything in my life—almost to a fault. I made a pact with myself to never let pain be a reason for not doing something, or, for that matter, anything. It took time to reel myself back in and learn to let go of the fear and, in its place, embrace self-love. Just because I can do things doesn't mean I should.

A comical yet heart-wrenching thing about living in

the TV room was that, for many months, I was unable to use a regular toilet. I could only transfer myself to a rolling toilet seat with a bucket under it that sat right next to my bed, and I had to have someone's assistance wiping my ass. It was truly humbling to have to poop right in the middle of the room and wait for whichever sibling was willing to wipe my butt. I felt like such an incredible burden on everyone. Someone always had to sleep near me in case I had to go to the bathroom.

One evening after I was freshly home from the hospital, my sister was on overnight duty. I had to pee, but I couldn't wake her and she was sleeping on the couch just out of arm's reach. I tried waking her many times. I tried to be polite, but nothing was working. I tried throwing a pillow at her, but she didn't budge. I was getting frantic. I yelled several times. Nothing. I had no other choice. So I just let go. Warm pee trickled down the side of my bed and pooled up my back. I just lay there, knowing that the consequences weren't going to be fun. But what else does a girl do? I laid there the remainder of the night, shivering as the warmth vanished. What set in was guilt, shame, frustration, and relentless itching. It was a long night and even longer next day. I had to transfer to the couch, very painfully, while the arduous task of cleaning the hospital bed was thrown upon my mother. Sorry, Mom, for everything, and thank you for everything.

I don't speak enough of my mother in this book. My story with her is still unfolding. Most of my life, my mother was pregnant and had babies, so her attentions were on the younger children. I believe one of the gifts that came from my accident was the time I got to spend with my mother getting to know her better. I had always been a daddy's girl, and I felt a little too raucous for Mom. What she had to deal with during the time of my injury makes her a saint in my book, and this is my book! Not once did I ever feel a burden to her. Never did I feel ashamed of my injuries or embarrassed by the many tasks for which I relied on her deeply: changing the dressings of my weeping wounds daily, bathing me, lifting me on and off the toilet and then having to expel the excrement, and the intense, excruciating physical therapy. Making the hour drive one way to and from doctors' appointments, all while caring for a newborn and a toddler at the same time. Mother carried the load of my accident emotionally and physically, taking care of my daily needs with grace, dignity, and the utmost, gentle love.

By the time December rolled around, it had been three long months since my accident. I could sit in a wheelchair for about an hour at a time. It was an excruciating hour, but I could do it.

My parents were urging me to go to the winter ball. I had been doing all of my school work at home with a tutor. Our home was 45 minutes from the school and out of town. So I hadn't seen many of my friends. Even my friends who lived nearby were busy with their senior year schedules, so they didn't get to come by that often. I was nervous at just the idea of going to the dance, of being away from home that long. What if I couldn't do the transfers in the bathrooms, what if my legs started hurting and I needed to lie down? What was I going to do while everyone else was dancing?

I didn't really want to face my peers. Last time they'd seen me, I had just been crowned homecoming queen. It all seemed a little overwhelming, but the urgency from my parents, teachers, and church leaders for me to get back out there was real, so I did. My mom ordered me a new outfit: long, wide-legged, velvet stretch pants to fit over the hardware on my legs; a green, velvet crocheted shirt; and a black, velvet tank top. She took me to get my hair done at the beauty salon—and even sitting that long in the salon chair made me think I wasn't ready to go to the dance. It was very, very painful, but I put on a good smile because I knew the effort my mother had made to get me out and about. I was on my way.

My friends met me at the front of the school and lifted me from the van into the wheelchair. My heart was racing. I was so nervous. My wounds were still healing, and my legs still had the halos, so every time my pulse quickened, I could feel it surging through every stitch, each metal rod and screw. Here I was. Who was I now? What was I now?

There is a Japanese tradition called kintsugi, the art of fixing broken things with gold. The philosophy is to treat broken or shattered objects with beautiful golden inlay rather than disguising the damage or throwing them away. I wish I had known then that my physical body, emotional self, and broken heart were filling up with so much gold, so much treasure, wisdom, and worth. That with all the damage, I was becoming so valuable I would never question my existence, worthiness, or purpose again, but instead revel in them. That one day I would walk around with my golden cracks illuminating my very core, a masterpiece of flawed, imperfect art. If I'd only known....

The dance was uncomfortable, uneventful, and awkward, just as I had thought it would be. It was hard for me to see my peers. Most of them didn't know what to say or how to approach me. I'm sure I wore my pain heavy in my eyes and on my heart. The very outgoing, loud-laughing, wild girl that had once inhabited my body was now replaced by an unsure, insecure, timid, and lost soul hanging on by a very thin and unravelling thread. What was also very uncomfortable was my family had started the preliminary inquiries of a lawsuit against the school, so I could sense the judgment from my teachers. It was like they were already getting ready to defend their position. The opposing sides were readying for war, and I was the pawn of proof for all of their justifications. I felt I didn't belong anywhere, in any room, or even in my body.

The rumblings of the lawsuit sent a shockwave through our small town. So many people with opinions, most of them thinking they knew better than me, my parents, or the school. They would have done something differently had the accident happened to them. They would have landed differently. They would have not jumped from as high. They would have thought before they jumped. Funny how it's always so clear to the people who weren't actually involved what they would have done in any given situation. I love this quote from Plato: "Opinion is the medium between knowledge and ignorance."

There is something strong and powerful about first-hand experience, and we should listen to those who have it. Should you ever find yourself caught up in gossip, privy to the "talk of the town," consider, instead of putting your energy into what you would have done better or differently, simply being grateful whatever it was didn't happen to you and that you don't have to be bothered with figuring it out. There is grace in allowing someone to learn their lessons in whatever manner the universe has granted them to do so, and even more grace in learning for yourself because of them. We don't all have to experience each other's suffering. We can surrender our need to be right, our egos and our insecurities, to compassion, empathy, and the unknown. It is a lesson I have had to learn several significant times in my life. How deeply the sharp words of another can wound us forever.

After trekking out for the winter ball and all that came with it, I retreated even more. I didn't want to see people. I didn't want to go to town. I was getting significantly more depressed. Wyoming winters are incredibly long in the best of times, but having to experience them from a hospital bed made it gruesome. The most recent surgery they'd performed on my right ankle was still not taking, and now there was a severe bone infection to contend with. My doctors warned me that if the infection spread and got worse, it could mean the amputation of my right leg from the shin down. That was terrifying news. I didn't want to feed into the drama—I really never felt like that was going to be my reality—but it did send my spirits plummeting.

My father was sensitive to my emotions. He could tell I was waning in the strength to keep my chin up. One morning, he woke me early and said, "I'm taking you to the ranch." I was very reluctant. Our ranch was not open to vehicles during the winter, and you could only snowmobile in and out. Nothing at the ranch was accessible for those with physical handicaps. The ranch was barely accessible to people with working legs.

I had noticed that being immobile and relying on everyone else to help me had created a lot of anxiety. What if something were to happen to Dad and I couldn't get out, or no one was around when I needed to go to the bathroom? It sounds silly now, but back then, those were valid fears I faced daily. The ranch seemed like the stuff of dreams: longed for, but also scary.

My father gathered up all my stuff: the transfer potty chair, the wheelchair, my bag of meds. He threw together a bag of pajamas—my only attire at the time—and then he scooped me up out of the hospital bed and away we went, up the snowy, slick staircase that led from the house to the cars. The biting cold air took my breath away and seemed to chill me through every metal rod, screw, and mesh that was newly located in my body. I closed my eyes and listened to the crunching of snow under Dad's heavy steps. The winter silence comforted me, and I was grateful to be outside for a moment. We trekked over the winding, icy corners of Towgwotee Pass in the Chevy half- ton, my bed made up on the narrow back seat. We listened and sang along to the local country western station.

The closer we got to the ranch, the more my anxieties subsided. The ranch had always been a haven for me, but I didn't know how it would feel now, in the new me. Would I feel as free even though confined to this chair? Would my heart still soar even though being heavy with despair? I was afraid to confront how I would accept my new self at my safe place. Could I welcome myself there?

At the ranch, it was even colder. The wind whipped about, slamming the doors of the truck. Dad made me another little bed in the back of the snowmobile trailer and piled all the stuff we had brought on top of me. With a quick tug on the pull rope, the snowmobile was running. Dad sat up front driving, with me in the back dodging the snow chunks that came pummeling at me from the tracks on the sled.

It felt so good to be out having an adventure! For a quick moment, my legs weren't hurting, and I didn't have a life-threatening bone infection. I was just a young girl out playing in the snow. I closed my eyes, letting the cold wind bite my cheeks. The scent of sweet pine sent me reeling back, and I imagined myself brand new—not the way I used to be, but a brand new me: upright, strong, beautiful, and walking—no, running!

I was quickly jolted back to reality when we came

over a bump that was much bigger than it looked. The snowy crest slammed into the base of the sled, and I felt every shattered bone in my legs jiggle. I almost barfed from the pain. Dad quickly shut off the snowmobile at the lodge and came running back, apologizing. "Honey are you okay? Sorry, that came out of nowhere."

That quick jolt grounded me right back to the depth of my reality, followed by a return of the sinking depression.

We set up my little hospital corner of the lodge, where I spent the rest of the afternoon watching music videos on CMT and stuffing brochures. This was before long email lists. Back in those days, you had to do your marketing and advertising by way of good, old-fashioned snail mail. I spent countless hours stuffing brochures with our new revised price list, then stuffing them into their addressed envelopes and sorting them into their designated zip codes. This job was perfect for someone who couldn't walk away by themselves.

After Dad stayed very late so I could make it without needing the bathroom, I spent the rest of the night in the old, huge, haunted lodge by myself (there used to be a graveyard on the property), on a little bed on the couch. All night I could hear the scurried scratching of determined mice gathering goodies off the floor, and all I could think about was them crawling up on me. Yuck!

I hardly slept, so when Dad came in the next morning early and said he had a present for me, I wasn't at all excited, just exhausted. I could tell from the way he stepped and the high tone of his voice that he was truly excited, so I got myself ready as best as I could by myself but needed help putting on new pants.

"Dad," I called, "can you help me put on my pants?"

"Oh, sure, honey. Sorry I forgot." He leaned down to reach my pants, which I'd gotten halfway up my legs, and we touched foreheads. I put my arms around his big, freshly shaven neck, the strong smell of bay rum freshly splashed on it. He lifted me, tugged my pants the rest of the way up, and set me gently back down on the couch.

"You ready now?"

And I was. I lifted each leg with my hands and set them over the side of the couch. The dangling always hurt. He kneeled down, and I slumped over onto his back, piggyback-style. With a slight groan, we were up and moving, past the office, past the big room warm from a crackling roaring fire. He opened the big front door, which was cumbersome, and we headed back out into the white, fresh, chilly morning.

"Where we going, Dad?"

"You'll see."

As we made our way across the ranch, I heard faint whinnying, which was very unusual, especially this time of year with five feet of snow on the ground and all the horses down south at the winter pasture. But I know I heard a horse as Dad stepped in the deep snow, his breath heavy from the weight of both of us.

We rounded the corner from the ranch house, and there at the corral was my beautiful mare, Marilyn. She had been a gift from Dad after I lost Tinkerbell in the lawsuit over our first ranch. I'd named her after Marilyn

Monroe, and she was so stunning that everywhere we went—rodeos, parades, any public place—people would always ask me if they could buy her. She was tall, half-Arabian and half-quarter horse, a bay paint with a long, white mane laid against black and brown patterns. She was fast, sassy, strong, and beautiful. As we approached her, I felt my heart breaking open. I immediately started crying, my tears freezing quickly to my cheeks.

Dad whispered, " I think it's time for you to ride."

He walked up close to her side, turned around, and gently hefted my butt up on the saddle. I grabbed the horn nervously, then he helped place each of my legs on either side of her while I did an awkward balancing act. As I sat atop her with halos protruding, she spooked at first and jumped a little sideways. Dad grabbed her. I just sat heavy in the middle. My emotions were all over the place, but the first big wash of emotion that came over me was pride. I had forgotten what it felt like to be tall: to stand tall, to rise above, to see above. Six months had passed since I had been upright with my legs beneath me. I was a little dizzy, my heart racing, and I was feeling a little woozy, "Dad, I'm gonna pass out."

"It's okay, honey-girl."

As if Marilyn had read my mind, she stepped out, and, with each movement forward, I regained my confidence. There was the slight smell of horse hair, crisp on the freezing air. I kissed at her, and she loped faster. I was free. She didn't care that I had once been a fast runner, a dancer, and a quick soccer player, and was now a mangled mess of pain. She knew me—my soul, my secrets,

71

and my quirks—and I, hers. She was ready and willing to be my legs. The undulating motion under me brought every inch of strength back to my spirit. I could be fast again. I could be free again. I could be tall. I could be me.

Dancing Queen

In that moment, riding Marilyn, I was able to shift into another frequency—a healing frequency. I believe it was the pure love from my horse that lifted me up and above my wounds and broken bones with the illuminous divine light of hope.

It was exactly a week from the day that I was able to ride again that my severe bone infection completely disappeared. Almost exactly a month later, I was able to stand on my own two feet (with the help of support bars and three physical therapists). Before, I hadn't actually been sure that I could pull out of the deep, fast nose dive my life had taken. My journey still seemed dark around me, but if I squinted, far down the road was a little ray of light, and, if I rode, I could get there a little faster. Marilyn had saved my life.

There's something mystical about women and horses. They just go together. It's as if the feminine human form is not actually complete without this captivating equine being. There's an essence of wildness and freedom that every girl has coursing through her veins, and somehow, when we ride, that wildness, that freedom, is tangible from the back of a horse. We are unstoppable. The primal sound of the hoofbeat drums us back to a time when our relationship first began, when the horse and the human thrived together. Entwined for eternity. This beautiful relationship still lingers for the cowgirl and her horse.

I spent the next several months focusing on healing. I still was not even close to being able to walk yet, but I was at least trying. I studied my school work hard, as college applications were all coming due and my senior year was coming to a close. I had planned on studying musical theatre, but given the extent of my injuries, I needed to change my focus. So between my parents, my choir teacher, and me, we decided that musical education would be the best bet for now. I applied all over. BYU, the University of Wyoming, Montana State, Utah State— just about every college in the west that was within an eight-hour radius from Jackson Hole. I knew I'd be in a wheelchair and needing to travel back and forth for surgeries and treatments.

There was still the dreaded lawsuit situation with the school, now getting more heated and starting to take off. I was still at home with a tutor because going to school was too much for my body, and the school day was too long to be sitting in a wheelchair. I was afraid for my future and feeling unsure how to move forward with college, but had learned from recent experience that it was much better to have goals and something to look forward to than to be stuck with the fear of not knowing my future.

I had never been a very patient person. I had also felt blessed in my earlier life with never really having to try very hard. Things came naturally and easily to me. Take the year I decided to play soccer. I knew nothing about it. I read a book on the way to our first game. But I was fast

and smart. By the end of the season, I was playing starting varsity as a sophomore.

All that had changed. I had to work really hard
at everything now. Nothing came easily. The simple
daily task of going to the bathroom and getting myself
dressed was at least a half-hour ordeal. Twenty years
later, I still have to modify the way I do things. Some
days I can hike three miles; other days, I barely can
make it to the bathroom without help because of such
severe osteoarthritis.

The days of being very good very fast were over. This
was a huge learning curve for me. Through the insight of
injury, I was learning patience and compassion, qualities
I had not necessarily embodied before the accident. I
joke that I'm a Mustang engine stuck in a golf cart body.
I've got a ton of get up and go, but the body just can't keep
up, so I still learn every day how to manage this body, my
greatest teacher.

At night, when my parents were sleeping, I would
make the daunting trek from my hospital bed to my
sitting chair, having to walk, crawl, and fall the ten feet
across the room. My doctors had ordered me to keep my
weight off my right ankle, but I felt like if I waited much
longer, I might never be able to walk again. Some nights I
would make it to the chair and not have enough strength
to make it back to the bed. Some nights I would not make
it to the chair at all, and my parents or a sibling would
find me sprawled on the floor and waiting patiently for
them to help transfer me back to bed.

I had to work really hard at finishing my school work

so I was able to graduate. I'm not sure if it was the head trauma from the accident or the fog of lots of pain medicine or just not being that invested in school anymore, but everything was laborious and slow.

As graduation neared, the school asked for kids to audition to perform at the graduation ceremony. I knew I could still sing—that was one thing that hadn't changed. So I asked Mom to load up the wheelchair and me, and we headed down to the school for the auditions. I got there and sang my heart out, feeling proud and excited that I could still do one thing well.

Weeks went by, and I never heard from the graduation committee. So I called and asked them if I was to perform. The answer was no.

Shit, this cut me down so hard. Why? Why? Was my song not good enough? Was it too painful for you people to see me in a wheelchair singing? Was it because my parents had decided to sue the school district? I went back to the school and begged them to let me sing. I told them that I wanted to leave school on a literal high note. I wanted my last memory of the school gym, the place that had changed my life, to be one I was in control of. A memory that I was proud of. I cried, I screamed, and finally they said I could perform a song at graduation. It seemed like a little battle won.

Because we lived so far from town and I was dependent on someone else to drive me, I missed all the graduation ceremony practices, so I didn't even tell anyone what I was going to sing. On graduation day, I showed up in a cap and gown and on crutches. My left leg was strong enough by this time to carry my weight for a very limited amount of time, and I wanted to stand at graduation instead of wheel in. A friend walked in with me—actually, he gave me a piggy back ride down the aisle to our seats.

There were the usual speakers, the fun videos of all the students, the pictures of them from when they were young, and then the senior portraits. I remember vividly when my picture came up. I didn't have a senior portrait because when they were taken, I was fighting for my life in a hospital. The photo that I had chosen to put in its place was a picture of me in a beautiful, lush green meadow in front of my favorite mountains, The Pinnacles, riding Marilyn. That is the image I wanted to be remembered by.

The ceremony commenced, and soon it was time for me to sing. They announced my name, and a sudden hush fell over the crowd in the gymnasium as I made the short trek up to the piano. It was only about 20 feet, but it seemed as if I had to go 100 miles to get to the edge of the piano. My crutches clip-clopped on the wooden floor. I never knew a room full of thousands could be so silent. I could hear only my pounding heart and quick nervous breaths. My dear and amazing teacher Bill was waiting to accompany me on the beautiful, black baby grand. I leaned against it as he gave me a quick smile and a wink. The rich tones reverberated through my body as he lightly played out the intro. I closed my eyes. I was singing for me. I knew this song and the message that I needed to send. I took a full breath, then released.

One hand Reaches out
And pulls a lost soul from harm
While a thousand more go unspoken for
They say what good have you done
By saving just this one
It's like whispering a prayer
In the fury of a storm
And I hear them saying you'll never change things
And no matter what you do it's still the same thing
But it's not the world that I am changing
I do this so this world will know
That it will not change me
This heart
Still believes
The love and mercy still exist
While all the hatred rage and so many say
That love is all but pointless in madness such as this
It's like trying to stop a fire
With the moisture from a kiss
And I hear them saying you'll never change things
And no matter what you do it's still the same thing
But it's not the world that I am changing
I do this so this world will know
That it will not change me
As long as one heart still holds on
Then hope is never really gone
I hear them saying you'll never change things
And no matter what you do it's still the same thing
But it's not the world that I am changing
I do this so this world we know

Never changes me
What I do is so
This world will know
That it will not change me

> ~ "The Change,"
> by Garth Brooks

I finished the song and slammed down into the piano seat. I could not stand another second. The room was still totally silent—not even the usual restless little kid sounds. I didn't know what to feel. Maybe I was that horrible? I thought I had sung purely from my heart with true and vulnerable emotion. But silence still. It seemed as though an hour had passed. I felt scared and unsure. I knew I had to make it back to my seat. I wanted to crutch proudly back, even though I had no idea what was going on in the minds of every silent person there. So I stood, and when I did, the entire gym stood with me and they were all screaming, yelling, and cheering me. This, this was everything to me. So thank you, people. For showing up for me that day when I needed you so deeply. Thank you thank you thank you.

CHAPTER FIVE:

Chrysalis

Trying to navigate my freshman year of college from a wheelchair was anything but a wild party.

I moved to Laramie, Wyoming, at the end of August. I had received many scholarships for music and art from the University of Wyoming, and I couldn't wait to get there. I was anxious to get away from the drama of my senior year, to get away from the doctors and surgeries, and even to get away from Mom and Dad.

Despite the fact that I was in a wheelchair, I was damn well going to drive myself to college. I got some help loading up my Ford Taurus. I had taught myself how to drive with my left foot, as to this day, my right foot doesn't flex or point, making it difficult to operate the accelerator. With my wheelchair handy, I sped off into the sunrise, eastern Wyoming-bound with the wind pushing back at me the whole way.

I moved into a split-level, incredibly inaccessible apartment with two girls who were both older than me. As those first weeks passed, I was still battling severe bouts of debilitating depression. Living through some tough times, I had felt the weight of depression before. But luckily I was born with an almost naïve positive attitude, and never before had I felt the physical symptoms of depression. Some days I couldn't get myself out of bed. I couldn't lift my arms or my head. The thought of feeding myself food was overwhelming.

On top of all this, my body was changing. I felt completely out of control in every aspect, physically, emotionally, and spiritually. I couldn't positive-think my way through this. It was as if I had to accept the depth of my thoughts and circumstances: settle there with them, find my bearings in the abyss of darkness, and begin to blindly coax myself back toward the light by feeling my way along. I literally had no clue who I was, how to be me, or where to start trying to find out. There were times I didn't actually leave the apartment for days or weeks, let alone leave my room.

Then came one blustery day with winds of what felt like 600 miles an hour. I had recently come back from Jackson after yet another operation on my legs. It felt like I was on surgery number 100. My surgical incisions were still fresh, but I needed to go to class to keep my scholarships. So I crawled from my downstairs bedroom, grabbed my wheelchair by the door, and, carrying it on my back, scooted myself on my butt out of the apartment, down four steps, and to my car.

Wriggling my frozen door open, I hefted the heavy wheelchair into the passenger's side, grabbed the steering wheel, and lifted myself into the driver's seat. After I coaxed the cold engine into starting, I drove off to campus, wishing I had some help or someone to be with. I pulled into the first handicap parking spot available.

I knew it was slick out, but had no idea to what degree. When I opened the car door and schlepped my wheelchair out onto the frozen tundra, it immediately slid across the barren ice of the parking lot, whisked away by the Wyoming wind. In horror, I watched as the chair took on a life of its own and went sliding further and further away, maybe 300 yards.

If you don't know what I mean by Wyoming wind, there is none compared to that of Laramie in winter. I started crying and cussing. I was hurting, and there wasn't a soul in sight. I could barely see, because at this point a full-blown blizzard was raging. I started to crawl to retrieve that which was serving as my legs. The pressure on my incisions from being in that position was excruciating. I was slipping, and my reaction to that was to shove my foot down to catch myself, but then the pain would tear up my legs. I tried scooting again on my rear, which eventually just turned into slipping uncontrollably toward my chair and hoping that no one would drive into the parking lot and be unable to stop.

I caught it. Or, at least, I put my hands on it. I tried getting into it from the ground, but there was so much ice it was like I was in the middle of a ridiculous Charlie Chaplin sketch. I ended up finally just dragging myself and chair across the slippery pavement toward the music building where my class had begun 15 minutes earlier.

At the bottom of the wheelchair ramp into the building, I braced my chair against the front of my car and was able to finagle my way up into it. But the chair started wheeling and pulling. I fought the chair, maneuvering through the ice and snow and progressing five feet forward only to slip back ten.

Soon enough, some nice human came along, saw my awkward predicament, and graciously gave me a nice push up the ramp and through the door. I was relieved and embarrassed at the same time, but also deeply happy to be in a warm building instead of freezing my ass off out in the snowbank.

I wheeled myself down the long hallway to the classroom. I was drenched, and the wheels squeaked with every rotation. Finally, I arrived at the classroom door, which was wood with a very small window out of my reach. I turned the knob. Locked, dammit! I knocked on the door. No one came. I knocked harder. Still no one. Wheeling back five feet, I slammed the front of my chair into the door to be heard. A pleasant enough girl unlocked the door but didn't open it.

Now for those of you who have never been in a wheelchair, let me help you understand the impenetrability of a solid wooden door. I tried opening it. Twice. Too heavy. I tried again, but barely got the footrest of my chair in between the frame and door. I swung the door with all my might and got the middle of the chair in before it came slamming back.

I could now see the faces of all 100 students staring at me. The ruckus I'd created had been going on for five minutes, but felt like eternity. Swinging the door once again with a squeak and grunt, I flung myself and my chair into the classroom. Sadly, the only handicap-accessible way to enter the main part of the room was down front where the teacher stood in front of tiered seating. So I made my way across the stage front and over to where the wheelchair seating was, realizing at the same time that I had left my backpack in the car. No books, no pencil, just me in my sopping wet clothes with my icy wheelchair and no pride left whatsoever. Every eye was on me.

I finally got settled and the teacher began speaking again. I felt a light tap on my shoulder, and then a sweet voice behind me said, "I think you're bleeding." I looked down in horror to see my bandages weeping with blood. Then I looked to where I'd just come from and saw that the entire stage was streaked with a trail of my blood—a significant enough amount to make everyone in the room uncomfortable. I just started laughing and crying at the same time. The entire rest of the class, all the students, left, and the teacher called the janitor and asked me if I needed the nurse. I declined and headed back down the trail of blood, sweat, and literal tears toward the car and what, at that point, I hoped would be my icy death.

I spent the rest of the afternoon crying in my bed. This would be true of most of my freshman year. On the outside, I was all positivity and forward motion. But inside, the struggle of acceptance was debilitating, so now not only was I struggling physically but my emotions were keeping me bedridden too.

83

I didn't know how to be this person. I didn't know how to just keep moving and pretending that everything was hunky dory. I was grateful that I was moving and semi-walking, but I didn't know how to do this in-between part. I was gaining weight, but it wasn't from the typical partying and drinking beer that produced the "freshman 15," it was from deep depression and not having a plan. How to work it out? Whose job was that? Should that have been something my parents did? Or my physical therapist? I had seen occupational therapists, but none of it seemed helpful. Too clinical.

Remember those aptitude tests we all took in elementary school? Well, ever since I was little, I scored the same damn thing on those tests. Every damn time. An entertainer, a musician. This was my destiny. But I had no idea how to do that now, or where I fit in. I had changed my major to become a music teacher, I had accepted this. I was even okay with it. But I was not happy.

At the University of Wyoming, there was a musical theatre group that I wanted to audition for. If you were accepted, you would spend time traveling and performing in shows around the country and in competitions. I wanted to be in it so bad, but on the audition sheet it asked those auditioning to prepare a couple of numbers to sing and to be ready to learn a 16-count dance piece.

I knew the dance part was out for me, so I decided to speak to the director of the musical theatre department. I wheeled myself to the music building, found his office, and knocked on the door. With a quick reply, I was ushered into his office. I introduced myself:

"Hi, my name is Jessica Garnick, and I would like to audition for the musical theatre group."

He gave me a full body scan up and down and said, "I'm sorry, it has a lot of movement and dancing, so I don't think it will be suitable for you."

And as quickly as I was ushered in, I was ushered out.

I was crushed. As I made the wheeled trek back to my car, I shed some tears, said some dark expletives, and then, just as suddenly as the emotions had welled, they slipped away. I decided to audition anyway. They didn't have to take me, but at least they would hear me.

I spent the next week singing, singing, singing and studying the songs I was going to perform for the audition. As the day grew closer, I got more and more excited. It felt so good to have a focus besides my legs or surgery. I enjoyed diving deep into the practice. I was feeling ready and rehearsed.

I woke up early that day and dressed myself in my most fancy hardware-friendly clothes, which I believe were fresh 90s wide-leg black velvet pants with a matching black velvet tank and a green crocheted velvet yarn sweater—the same outfit I had worn for the winter ball. Yes, I know. H.O.T.

I threw my wheelchair in the trunk, crawled my way to the front of the Ford Taurus, and zipped off to campus. Earlier that week, I had signed up for the last audition spot available. I wanted to leave an impression. I made my way down the long hallways with the familiar sounds of my wet wheelchair squeaking its way to our destination. At the door, I stopped, took a deep breath, and said a prayer asking God to give me extra courage and strength.

85

I hefted the heavy door open, slid my chair in with the usual slamming of it two times to get through, and wheeled my way across the dark black box theatre to the edge of the piano. I stood up on my one better leg, leaned upon the piano, introduced myself, handed my music to the pianist, and told him to play and not to stop until I said to. Beautiful notes came from the piano. I fell deep into the tones and sang, sang like I have never before in my life without care, judgment, or fear. I sang:

I could be in someone else's story
In someone else's life and they could be in mine
I don't see a reason to be lonely
I should take my chances further down the line,
And if that girl I knew should ask my advice,
Oh I wouldn't hesitate, she needn't ask me twice!
Go now, I'd tell her that for free, trouble is the girl is me
The story is, that girl is me

> ~ "Someone Else's Story,"
> by Benny Goran, Bror Andersson,
> Bjoern K. Ulvaeus, and Tim Rice

I must have had an immense amount of power around me that day, because I sang like I had never sung before. I was weeping, but I made it through the song with such emotion and such power that when I finished, the room was silent. I collapsed into my wheelchair—it had taken everything I had to stand that long. As I looked up, I saw that the four people in the room, including the pianist, were all crying. Then they stood up and cheered for me.

I felt satisfaction, accomplishment, and love. I gratefully thanked them and squeaked my way back across the long, wooden floor.

A week passed. I had just finished my music theory class when my friend came up to me and said, "You missed rehearsal."

I didn't know what she was talking about.

"What rehearsal?" I asked.

"For the musical theater group," she said.

"I didn't get in."

"Yes, you did."

She took me to the bulletin board, and there was my name, Jessica Garnick, among about 15 other students. The notice said, "Congratulations. You've made it into Musical Theatre and Dance Ensemble. Thank you to everyone who auditioned."

That was a HUGE DAY! I felt so grateful to myself for not being afraid. For listening to my spirit that was telling me to sing, because that is still something I can do, and love to do. For not listening to the department head and for taking a chance anyway, knowing going in that they wouldn't take me. I was beginning my own metamorphosis. Looking back, I wish I could have had the insight to see that life had broken me open so that I could start my chrysalis, that sac in which the larva (caterpillar) transforms into a butterfly. The chrysalis makes the larva immobile. This process is very intense and painful. The insect's little body liquifies from its own digestive fluids, and the body is restructured using specialized formative cells. This is a process called histogenesis, in which undifferentiated cells are used to build different body tissues, similar to what happens when humans make their own stem cells. Yes, I had begun my chrysalis and was in process. I was resting still, immobilized and turned inward, but this would allow me to get quiet and find the healing on a cellular level that I would need to one day fly.

CHAPTER SIX:

Trail or Trial

T he aftermath of my accident brought a nasty, litigious battle between the school system and me. I had only been 17 for about a month on October 29, 1997, the date of my accident, but by the time we filed the lawsuit the next fall, I had turned 18. Suddenly, as an adult, this became my lawsuit against the school, even though I had no idea what that entailed or even meant. When I say "accident," I throw it out there because I don't really know what to call it. When you refer to an accident, people assume a car accident. When I tell them I was doing an obstacle course, they jump to the conclusion that I was horseback riding. Then I tell them that I was doing an obstacle course in my senior year of high school P.E. class, and that after I jumped from a second story, the mat slipped out, and I landed on the hardwood gym floor, shattering both my lower extremities, and breaking my cheekbones and my nose. The conversation proceeds:

"Wait, you jumped?"

"Yes."

"Why?"

"Ummm, I had to do the obstacle course in order to get a grade in that class."

"That's bullshit, I hope you sued the hell out of them."

"Yeah."

"Did you win a ton of money?"

"No."

Thus began the infamous tale of Jessica Garnick vs. Teton County School District. The lawsuit of whose fault it really was. Who was to blame? Me? The school? My shoes? The gym floor? Mercury in retrograde? That was the major question for the courts.

My trial didn't begin until the fall of 1999, two years later than the "incident"—in fact, the anniversary of it. Two years of healing, suffering, walking and not walking, schooling, ranching, singing, crying, growing, and trying to survive the in-between.

Little did I know that my every move was under great scrutiny during those two years building up to my trial. The trial process was very long and harsh and, for me at such a young age, terrifying.

There's a specific process. First, you have to decide to file a lawsuit. Next, you file complaints with the courts known as pleadings, which explain each side of the parties' dispute. Then comes discovery, the longest part of the case. That's when both sides spend time gathering information and evidence and interviewing witnesses. Next is the conclusion, when there is hopefully a settlement in which both parties agree to resolve the conflict without going to trial.

My case went like this. In the early spring of 1998, a few months after I was injured, my parents, after much counsel, decided that we should sue the school. They didn't have the money or insurance to cover the massive hospital bills, and they just wanted help—they'd even consulted with the school on the decision to go ahead and sue them. I don't believe anyone had truly considered the consequences of this process. I recall having a conversation with my parents about the decision to move forward with the lawsuit in which we thought that the legal proceedings would be brief, and we could probably settle out of court.

At first, that seemed to be true. I went on with my new routine of trying to walk and figure out my new life routine—until we started depositions. Depositions, which take place during discovery, are oral or written testimonies given under oath but not in a courtroom. Usually, they take place in the office of either participating attorney. Everything changed for me the day they started.

It was a beautiful summer morning, the sun peeking over the Pinnacle Mountains. A light, pine-scented summer breeze had kicked up, sending new breath through the deep green grass of the Wind River Valley and giving life to the day ahead. Cowboys, horses, dogs, and people hustled about the ranch, readying themselves for whatever adventure was planned. Dad seemed anxious as he picked me up in front of my cabin. He was a big man, 6'2", broad-shouldered, fit, and movie-star handsome. He

91

drove his truck not unlike the way he rode his horse: both hands on the steering wheel and rocking back and forth at the pace of a quick trot. His signature move. Anyone who knew him knew this about him, his funny little driving quirk. But today, his rocking was a little quicker—heavier and more intense.

"Dad, you okay?"

"Honey-girl," he said, "it's a big day. They aren't going to let me in the room with you. So you have to speak your truth. Don't be afraid. Know I love you."

His words were thought-out and direct. It was a long drive over the pass as worry began to set in. Was this a big deal? Why all of a sudden did I feel scared? The usual stunning scenery seemed muted compared to the heaves of worry and anxiety I was now experiencing. Dad slowed the car in front of an obscure building across the street from the local cop shop.

"Is this it?" I asked.

"We're here," he sighed.

He came around my side of the truck, opened the door for me, and held out his strong arm for me to take, looping mine through his. This was the way we walked most of the time—partially because we were close, but mostly because he knew I needed the extra support on my feet. We entered the building, and I saw for the first time the attorneys who were representing the school. One looked to be in his late 30s: young, clean-cut, Wyoming raised, and not conventionally handsome. He had a fresh, aggressive face and an ego-swollen jaw. The other attorney was a red- haired, tight-lipped woman whose belly was swollen from being six months' pregnant; you could sense the heaviness of her job and her pregnancy with her every sigh as she climbed the stairs.

We all shook hands. I could feel my father's anger vibrating from his every cell. His demeanor was pure, old-fashioned cowboy—he'd rather have just kicked the shit out of every person in the room and called it even. The old eye-for-an-eye mentality. My father waited outside the room anxiously as I sat through eight hours of questioning, with distorted truths, leading and misleading statements, and rants coming from both sides of the legal equation.

I was in depositions for three days, all of them ranging from grueling to downright depressing. Each night, when we were finished, I would fall asleep in the truck on the way home and only wake up long enough to crawl into bed. I'd sleep until Dad knocked on the door of my 100-year-old cabin that sat on the banks of the Wind River at our ranch– nothing fancy, but I loved having my own little space that I shared with two of my friends who worked with me at the ranch. You could see daylight through each log, and know already from the cracks in each, what the weather outside was doing.

I was slipping back into familiar, deep, dark territory. Depression's unwelcome walls were too high to see out of and closing in quickly on me. I knew this valley well now: the indifference and apathy, the hazy aloofness, the energetic void, the lack of appetite or ability to feel love. A ray of light glimmered at the narrowing end of the valley, but it seemed a million miles away with no way of getting there. My legs, eyes, and heart were too heavy to make the journey.

I learned hard truths for an 18-year-old during these times. The subject of truth was very perplexing. When I researched the definition of truth, this came up:

Truth:
(1): body of real facts,
(2): the state of being the case
(3): a transcendent fundamental or spiritual reality
(4): sincerity in action, character, and utterance.

I understood these statements completely. I tried to live them as well as I could. But the courtroom showed me a side of humanity I had never been exposed to or ever really wanted to know. I had seen blatant violence, disgust, evil, lies, and betrayal before, but I was about to experience all this from people I had once upheld in my church, in my school, and even among my friends.

It was during this time that I realized that truth for some people is not the same as truth for others. I had been taught that you tell the truth no matter who it hurt, even if that person was yourself. That there was only one truth. But my attorneys were telling me that truth was a perception, almost like an opinion. I can comprehend that, but that explanation is not my truth. My truth doesn't come with justifications or qualifications. It isn't slippery, and it doesn't slither in and out to suit whoever is telling it. My truth is ancient; it sits deep in the crevasses of every bone. When it is spoken, it is brave, like the tongue of the earliest languages, lost amongst man's ego and self-righteousness. My truth, when told, shakes the very earth and registers in the gut like a needle on the Richter scale. Conversely, when my truth goes unspoken or is misspoken, it rots and stinks of death, festering to the very core of the bones it sits in. So I must tell the truth because I cannot live with the disease that comes from lying.

We all have a choice to speak our truths, to radiate in pure glory and the freedom that doing so gives us, or to lie, and choose the rotting, moldering decay that comes with the falsehoods that eat away at our very core, leaving us depleted. I told the truth, but I learned quickly that I was not the norm. When people are afraid of truth, they make choices without understanding the consequences.

At first, it seemed like the proceedings were designed to find out the truth: Who was speaking authentically? Who was lying? But quickly, the focus became what had happened and who was at fault. And so we went from seeking truth to finding blame. Blame, it turns out, is a whole 'nother mind fuck.

Blame:
(1): to find fault with
(2): to hold responsible

This is the basis of every court proceeding in the US. The quicksand wash between truth and blame gets sticky, heavy, and deep while on the painful path to justice.

Three months after the depositions, there was still no agreement on a settlement. The insurance company and its attorney offered me a single dollar at the first settlement meeting. I believe it was this cocky young attorney's attempt to try and shake me and bully me, to make me feel insignificant and unworthy by offering such a paltry amount. It kind of worked, and you can imagine how throwing me went over with my family. My father was livid; I wanted this to all be over. I couldn't bear seeing my father depressed and furious all over again. My mother was quietly angry, lips pursed and lost in prayer.

Proceedings for the trial took place, and the opening moments established the nastiness that would come to characterize our case. This, I learned, is the usual path with most court cases. Whoever can fight the nastiest and the dirtiest prevails. It takes a certain kind of human to be a trial lawyer, but we need them and we need good ones.

Looking back, I wish we had taken that dirty dollar they offered, and I'd left it sitting on the table. I had no idea of the lion's den I was limping into. No amount of money can buy back your dignity. There is no silver dollar shiny enough to make you new again. But I didn't know these things yet. I was on the brink of my wisdom. I was learning. I was immersed slowly into the burning flame of what I came to call the un-justice system.

I had taken the fall of my sophomore year of college off to deal with the court case. My first day of court was spent sitting through the jury selection, listening to each prospective juror. "Do you know the plaintiff, Jessica Garnick?" they were asked. Most of them answered yes. The ones who didn't know me personally nonetheless knew my family, or went to church with us, or had a son or daughter in school with one of my seven siblings.

It took a painstakingly long time to find someone who wasn't acquainted with us or didn't have friends who were. This is the way of it in small towns. But somehow by the end of the day we had 12 jurors sworn to be fair, sworn to be unbiased, and sworn to be just.

That first day, I'd shown up in the clothes I'd normally wear to help out at the ranch. My attorneys quickly schooled me in the ways of proper court attire—my costume, as it were. I didn't know that the show was beginning. They want you to wear church dress, respect the court. Don't come in your everyday clothes. Look demure, be at your most attractive. As the trial went on, I realized how similar the court room was to live theatre. There was an audience, a judge, and jurors; there were actors, attorneys, and witnesses. This was all familiar to me. The only difference was that no one had told me I would be playing a part. And that my part was to flay open my life.

I would have never chosen to play this character. She was too deep, too heavy, too pained. And yet there I was at center stage, told to dance and sing like a marionette and being pulled apart from every direction. It was heart-wrenching, my trial, the stuff of movies, complete with tears, lies, deceit, pain, and suffering.

I was lost, unable to discern real life from court life or my truth from someone else's rehearsed script. The defendants were winning because I was breaking down. I couldn't stand listening to the teachers I'd loved,

97

trusted, and revered tell lies about me to save their asses. I knew—and they must have known—that I was injured for life. Why, I agonized, didn't they want to see me get better, even if it meant making sure my hospital bills were paid? By this time, I had begun walking occasionally with a cane, but I was still in and out of wheelchairs because of the ongoing surgeries being performed. My left leg was getting much better, but weight-bearing hurt, and I tired quickly.

Today, the fate of my right leg is still up in the air. The doctors have told me that my future probably holds two ankle fusions and then, gradually moving on up the leg because of the way I will have to walk and compensate, an eventual knee replacement followed by a hip replacement. But by the time of the trial, I could walk, at least some of the time. No matter the pain, walking meant everything to me. Still does.

These days, my mobility varies depending on my activity level. Some days, I don't need a cane; some days I need a wheelchair. The extent of my injuries was and is deceptive. If you were to see me walking down the street, you might not suspect anything wrong. But if you were to see me the next day, I might be back in the wheelchair and unable to walk at all. It is, I know, very confusing and difficult for others to understand.

One day, at the end of the first week in court, I was limp-walking without the use of a mobility device. This had been a week of draining days, emotional days, and lengthy court sessions full of twisted lies, painful remarks, false accusations, and torn hearts—mostly mine. My parents weren't allowed in the courtroom with me, so I faced all of the testimony alone.

A dear family friend and one of the most incredibly loving women I've ever known, Sharon Henrie, showed up every day and sat calmly near me. Her strong, stoic presence brought so much peace to me. She never said anything, but she knew I needed to know that I mattered to someone, and that was her. Thank you, Sharon. I love you.

This was a particularly hard day at court. I had just heard testimony from many experts that my injury was not going to be a big deal, that it would not affect my life, that I should be totally fine. It was my attorney's idea to show the court how I really walked to counter this testimony.

I did not want to do this. I didn't and still don't walk very well barefoot. I'm actually quite handicapped when I don't have shoes on or my orthotics in. My right foot is stuck in tiptoe, like a Barbie doll's, so while I can walk on my toes just fine, I can't walk flat-footed. What results is a jolting, staccato, up-down movement as I shift my weight from one slightly normal foot to the more disabled right foot with the pointed toe. I can walk easily in heels, and since I live in boots, I can fluidly move. I say that is divine synchronicity for this cowgirl.

On this day in court, I'd been asked several antagonistic questions by the defendants' attorney and listened to their experts insist I was just fine. Then it was my attorneys' turn.

They asked me to please remove my shoes and walk

for the jury. I slipped my cowboy boots off. It was unnerving to undress in front of the crowd. I knew how vulnerable I was about to be. I muttered a prayer and told myself to be brave. Barefoot, I started my shaky, crippled walk down the steps, between the spilt side of the courtroom, between the little swinging doors, and down the long, divisive aisle of room. I heard many whispers, a gasp, and even some slight whimpering.

I turned around because I was having pretty severe pain. The trek back seemed like a marathon, with all eyes on me and each gaze burning into my skin. Not many people made eye contact, instead looking down at my feet or turning their heads away from me as I passed. As I made my way back to the stand and slowly limped by the defendants' table, one of their attorneys, a red-headed woman, leaned to her partner and loudly whispered, "She's faking it."

I'm not sure if it was part of her plan for me to hear that, but hear it I did, and her plan worked. Those words crushed me all over again. Every recently shattered bone in my body echoed with the pain so intensely that I almost collapsed right there. I knew in that moment I couldn't let that heartless human win. With tears streaming down my face, I chose not to look over at her, but instead paused right by their table, closed my eyes, took a deep breath, and imagined I was back on my beautiful Marilyn riding the peaks of the Absaroka Mountains, the chinook wind blowing through my hair. Beyond this windowless courtroom with all the lies, greed, and hate that inhabited it.

That brief respite gave me strength enough to collapse back onto the stand, easing my way into my seat while trying hurriedly to put my boots back on. My humanity, my heart, my soul, my life's purpose, my truth, and my dignity had been questioned and torn apart to the point where I was starting to wonder myself what was real anymore. What was the truth? Who was telling the truth? Why were all these people who still had lives, the use of their legs, and a purpose so determined to invalidate mine? I didn't know anymore.

I just wanted to be done. I wanted to be living the life other 18-year-olds were. I wanted to be having careless college fun. Instead, I was listening to some of my dearest teachers tell lies about me. Having "experts" tell me that I was not that special, not that talented—so all of this didn't matter. These would become the darkest days of my life. I was being betrayed, lied to, and laughed at. I was the talk of the town. There were doctors to heal my legs, surgeons to carefully piece back together my body, and nurses to nurture me through rehabilitation—but who was going to heal my shattered heart?

The realization that I was the only one who could begin the long, arduous journey of piecing back together my hope, my trust, my confidence, my worth, my joy, and my strength was harrowing. That journey would become a daily spiritual ritual: some days, I'd win, and some days, I'd just feel like lying in the middle of the road while the rest of the world trampled over me.

The trial lasted for another week, by which time I'd shut down all emotion and built up an impenetrable wall

101

of self-protection so that whatever the outcome, it couldn't hurt me. My emotional armor was so thick, heavy, rigid and cold that no one nor anything could get in. What I didn't realize was that I would also be unable to get out.

I guess you could say the trial ended in my favor. The jury concluded that the school district and I were equally to blame. I was awarded $125,000 in damages, but after court and attorney fees, it came to less than half of that. I put the remainder in a bank account, and there I was, 19 years old by that time, with a broken body and $50,000. It wasn't enough to pay my hospital bills and not even close to enough to handle a future of living with lifelong disability. I should have gone to a financial planner to help me see how to work my money for the future, but I didn't. I blew through that money quicker than summer lasts in the Rocky Mountains. I gave my mom a loan, bought some new tack, and let the rest sit in a regular checking account.

It's painful to look back now and see that I could have made better choices, but I was still a kid, and I had no way to know the future. I was ashamed and overwhelmed, lost in an incredibly heavy fog of depression. Putting one mangled foot in front of the other and simply trying to stay on the trail of my new life was hard enough.

Interestingly, I've come to notice in general and especially while writing this book, I've misspelled trail and trial numerous times. Note:

Trial: a formal examination of evidence before a judge, and typically before a jury, in order to decide guilt in a case of civil proceedings.

Trail: a mark or a series of signs or objects left behind by the passage of someone or something. A beaten path through rough country, such as a forest or moor.

Each seem like the opposite end of the spectrum, yet they are both deeply intertwined in my life, weaving in and out of the weeks, the months, and the years. There is some comfort for me in knowing now that my trail led me through my trials, that my trials have been the trail. My father had a saying about riding horses on the trail, and it applies to life: "Keep your seat in the middle, your eyes to the skyline, and watch your top knot."

CHAPTER SEVEN:

Heartbreak and Horses

T his is where true real healing begins, the place where you learn to rise up again. Strap your heaviest baggage onto you. You might even have to drag it for a while, but always keep moving. Lifting that baggage makes you stronger. One day you will be strong enough to throw the weight into the stratosphere, but first you must feel it, rise with it, learn from it. Then, at the peak of divine timing, let it go, wish it well, be grateful for it, and then crawl, walk, run, fly—whatever you can do at the moment to keep going.

The year after my trial was still a little foggy and grey. I was beginning to walk a little better—at least, I didn't need the use of a walking aid as much—and I was riding a ton. I had wanted to get back into rodeoing, so my father and I were on the hunt for a barrel-racing horse. Our friends in Jackson had a lead. Enter Starbuck, a beautiful sorrel gelding and the first male horse I had ever bought and paid for outright on my own. He was fast, very powerful, and maybe, according to my dad, "a little too much horse" for me at the time, but I knew he was perfect. I wasn't walking well, but I could ride far as the day is long. We brought Starbuck home to the ranch, and I was beyond excited to start working with him.

I had other trials during that time besides the one happening in the courtroom. I had just come out of a very bad break-up that left my heart feeling as shattered as my legs. My first love, a year-long relationship that I'd begun at college with a guy from Oregon, had ended with a phone call from him telling me he "didn't want to come back to Wyoming." I was devastated. He had proposed to me earlier that year, which may sound young, but for a 19-year-old Mormon looking for love and safety, it had seemed like the answer to my prayers—and, for a while, it was. He was there for me, made me laugh, and thought I was pretty and fun at a time when I mostly felt I was neither. The seriousness of my accident and physical circumstances didn't seem to bother him. In retrospect, I'm not sure he even really understood them. At any rate, it turned out that he had other hearts to break. So I found my way back to myself with Starbuck.

The first time I tried running the barrels on Starbuck at home, I needed to move the barrels apart a little further apart for a regulation pattern. Barrel racing is a competitive rodeo event in which you complete a cloverleaf pattern around barrels pre-set in specific positions in the fastest time possible. At the collegiate and professional levels, it's primarily an event for women. It's a dance between horse and rider to safely and successfully maneuver around the big, 50-gallon barrels.

In a regulation-width pattern, the barrels have to be a specific distance from each other for a professional time qualification. I wanted to race professionally, so I needed to practice that way. One day, I had warmed up Starbuck in the arena, loping the length of the tall fence round and around to get him calm and ready, practicing lead changes and roll backs, stopping him on a dime, and then backing him up a couple of steps to make sure he was soft in my hands and listening to my subtle commands.

I leaned from my saddle to grab the barrel and move it. Suddenly, I felt the whole earth moving. He swallowed his head (meaning he went to bucking hard). I was hanging off on his right side, trying to get my ass back in the middle, but I was already off-balance from carrying the barrel.

I went to grab the reins to try to bring him around but kept sliding off the side. He was launching himself so hard, I could feel my stomach drop, like when you drive over a hill too fast. I knew he meant business.

I couldn't get back in the middle—in fact I was closer to the dirt than the horse's back—so I let go, slamming hard onto the arena floor, head and shoulder first. I got a mouthful of arena, a distinct mixture of dirt, sand, and horse shit. Trying to get my bearings, I looked up to see Starbuck's ass headed my way. I scrambled, but couldn't get out of the way quickly enough. His hind feet met with each of my ankles. SHIT! It hurt so bad! There was a familiar rush of blood to the injury site, and swelling began. I was afraid to try to walk, but I also didn't know if he was gonna land on me again, so I jumped (as much as I could jump up, anyway—probably it was more like a roll) and hurried out of the line of fast-moving hair, hooves, and snorting nostrils.

I was scared. Scared that I had reinjured myself. Scared that Dad was going to take Starbuck away. Scared that everything in my life was going south. Starbuck kept running around the arena as fast as I'd ever seen him run. I tried stopping him, but he blew past me again and again, barely missing me. I felt as though I was screwing everything up. I couldn't catch him. I could barely walk— again! I could feel the blood pooling in my joints, but I knew it was impossible to break metal, wire, screws, and plates. A sense of defeat came over me.

I made a decision. I knew I couldn't stay in that feeling of defeat for long without losing myself to it. So I sat in the middle of the arena, the cool, stirred-up earth under me. I took a deep inhale, the smell of sweaty horse and crushed sage filling my nose, and I let go. Let go of the idea of how this relationship between me and my new horse should be. Let go of the fear that my ankles were busted again. Let go of my idea of how my life was supposed to be, of my old boyfriend and the naive dreams I had conjured up with him. As I closed my eyes and listened, a slight breeze kicked up, and a dust devil blew through, the arena coating every inch of me with the soil I had been raised on. I heard the deep huffing of Starbuck's crazed panting as my saddle slapped a drumming beat against his tired body. Both sounds created my only anchor to the world outside my exhausted meditation.

I cried. Not out loud, but a couple tears streamed from the corner of my eyes, leaving a tiny trail of mud down my cheek, along my sore neck, and onto my dusty, torn shirt. Starbuck came to a halting stop. I could no longer hear the rhythmic pounding of hooves, only the wheezing of his breath. My eyes still closed, I stood up slowly, my legs still shaking, clumsy, like a newborn foal. There was a hot breath on my back, and I turned while opening my eyes to meet Starbuck face to face, both of us sweaty, tired, and discouraged. I calmly grabbed a rein and turned the stirrup toward me, stood straight on my strongest leg, and gently, painfully, ever so calmly swung my leg over—and once again, I was centered in the saddle.

Loping a couple more turns around the arena, I could feel adrenaline wearing off and pain settling in, and I knew that this moment contained lessons for both Starbuck and me. What does defeat mean to you? At this point in my life, it had so many meanings for me. Was life defeating me, or showing me grace? Was she sculpting me into a finely tuned instrument of raw, deep, humanity, carved with life experience?

Defeat. I looked up the word in several different places, most of the meanings: lost to opponent, failure to succeed or win. None of these definitions suited me. I did not nor ever had I given in to defeat. I had fleeting moments and emotions of defeat. But I had never dropped into the depth of defeat. I had clung to the side of it just as

I had hung off the side of Starbuck. Life had bucked me off, had left me clinging from its sides and barely hanging on, then had slammed me to the ground and crushed my physical body. But I was hell bent on getting back on and getting back up. My definition of defeat: when there is nothing else you can do but keep going.

After taking the fall off for the trial, I'd decided not to go back to college for spring semester. That decision held on through to the next year, and I didn't end up going back to college at all. I stayed at the ranch and continued healing. I did so by spending most my time riding, making new friends among the temporary employees who would come for the season, and trying to get back to a normal place and existence. My ability to walk improved, but I was still in an intense amount of pain. For a while it seemed I was living off of Aleve and any other anti-inflammatory I could get my hands on.

Finally, after a year of wheedling, coaxing, and fighting, I convinced my father to let me take over as head wrangler at our ranch. The duties entailed managing 100 head of horses, overseeing the breeding program of our 20 head of brood mares, being responsible for the care and upkeep of all tack, pasture management, and wrangling 15 employees (most of them cowboys). My father was not a typical cowboy in most ways, but he was still old-fashioned enough at times to question the abilities of women to handle jobs that men had been doing for centuries. I really wanted to prove myself. I had watched many men come into this position and I knew that I was more knowledgeable, better-qualified, and certainly eager.

I took my new role very seriously. I felt I did a damn good job too. Never had our herd been so strong, healthy, and viable. Our corrals ran smoother than ever, and the morale of the employees was at an all-time high. I knew that I had to be willing to do everything that I asked my guys to do. So that included riding the rank horses (broncs that like to buck or that are not yet broke in), even though I knew the toll it would take on my already damaged body. I could walk well enough, but I was best on horseback. I did my job, but every night, in the privacy of my cabin, I was icing and elevating my feet from the pain. The NSAIDS that allowed me to function also fostered dependency on them. I knew it wasn't a good thing, but my fear of missing out was once again strong. By this point, I could walk without assistance most of the time, but even with special orthotics to help minimize my limp, it was extremely painful. Still, walking in pain was far better to me than not walking at all, so I suffered silently, not wanting to give my energy to the struggle.

I have always loved being a cowgirl. There is a real romance in this lifestyle of living off the land. Consequences come hard and fast. You learn to develop a very heightened sense of awareness so you won't get your ass plowed into the dirt from whatever force you are dealing with, be it horses, humans, or nature. Trust me, it happens more often than not.

One morning, it was my turn to wrangle in the horses. Wrangling during early summer mornings was such a perk of the job. It was beautiful out, and the horses were fresh, though sometimes hard to find in our 1200 acres of woods and river bottom. That day, I had chosen to ride a very well-broke horse who was usually as honest as the day is long.

When you turn horses out to pasture on such wide open spaces, you usually bell them, which means that you put bells around their necks so that you can find them by hearing the ringing. It's especially important to bell the ones who are a little sneakier and hard to find, as well as the herd leaders. Horses have a herd mentality, and there is usually one we call a "bell mare." She's the one who leads the herd. Most of the other horses stick to her path and follow in her footsteps. You could say that she's the alpha of the horse herd.

There were always a little sneaky bunch of our oldest horses who knew all the tricks of the trade and did everything in their power to avoid being brought back to the ranch and saddled up for the greenest of dudes. That morning, with the birds singing and the Wind River burbling, I stopped my horse alongside the bank to take a listen. In the distance, I could sense the faint sound of bells. I hurried my steed into the chest-deep water, the cold freezing up my joints and stealing my breath. Bullseye, my horse for that morning, lunged out of the water and up onto the steep embankment. I don't know if it was the cold water, the brisk morning air, or the motion of lunging over the dead timber that was blocking our trail to the top, but suddenly Bullseye swallowed his head and started bucking. He hadn't done this since he was a colt, and it caught me off guard. We were midair, and I could see that all four of his hooves were off the ground. I knew we were going to hit hard. As Bullseye's hooves met the ground the impact slung me up over the saddle horn so that I was riding on his neck. Just at the peak moment, as he was getting momentum back for another spring, my face smacked into his poll, which is the pointy place right between a horse's ears. Sharp pain, then darkness.

I was hearing bells for sure now! As I shook off the ringing in my ears, my vision started to clear. Just then, a wet nose stirred me. I had landed among some downed timber, and Bullseye was sniffing me almost as if to say he was sorry. Everything was still. I lay for a while, scanning my body once again for damage done. It didn't seem too bad. My face was numb, but as I was already assuming that I had a broken nose, this was a familiar feeling. For some reason, I had decided to wear a white puffy vest that morning—let's be honest, white anything in this line of work was usually going to be black by the end of a day spent shoveling horse shit, saddling, and riding. Trying to regain my strength, I stood up, a little wobbly and my head spinning, and looked down to see that the front of my white vest was covered with blood.

Shit! I knew that my nose was probably broken and figured that was the source. At a snail's pace, I crept out of the dead timber to a place where I could get back on my horse. Adrenaline was the only thing driving me at this point. I knew I had to find the horses and get back to the ranch. Slowly and gently, I swung my leg back over Bullseye, keeping light in my stirrups in case we were going to have a replay, but he seemed to have gotten it all out if his system. I kicked him back up the deep timber to the sounds of the horses.

I heard a voice calling, "Heyyyyaaaawhooooooop," calling the horses home. It was a familiar, comforting sound, and I was grateful to hear it. At the ridgeline, I saw the silhouette of my little brother Creed herding the horses in. When I rode up on him, he immediately said, "What the fuck happened to your face?"

I tried to talk, but my lips were so tight I knew something was really off.

"Jess, your lips," Creed said.

I reached up to feel my face. It was really numb, and there was something in my mouth behind my teeth making it hard for me to talk. I stuck my finger in my mouth to figure out what it was, and realized that I had put my teeth through my top lip and some of my lip was still behind my teeth. With a sharp yank, I pulled my lip back down. I could feel the breeze on my open wound, painfully sharp, and I prayed that the wind would die down. The sting on my open wound brought tears to my eyes. At one point, I decided that it would be better to put my mangled lip back behind my teeth, so there wasn't this drooping gap, but my attempt to do so brought new pain.

Creed was only around 14 at the time, but he was so supportive. Having his presence by my side as we rode the half-hour back to the ranch gave me so much comfort. He held the space for me to be hurt and took charge so that I could just focus on getting home. He tried to make me laugh to keep my mind off the pain, reassuring me that I didn't look too horrible.

We made it back to the corral. I didn't want to be too much of a sissy, so I continued with my other duties, catching and saddling the 50 horses for the morning ride. But I was getting really tired, and my face was pounding along with my head. Delegating the rest of the chores, I headed in a little early to the breakfast room, where I immediately fell asleep.

I woke up to my dad shaking me.

"Jess, you okay? You look terrible."

"Yes, Dad, fine, just had a little run-in with my horse's head," I said, embarrassed.

"Dammit, Jess, you need to be more careful!" Like that was my fault. "We'd better get you to the doctor."

But it being about two hours now since the incident, I knew that there wasn't much they were going to do for me. Dad helped me to the car, and we made the 90-minute drive over Togwotee Pass to Jackson. I slept the whole time. The doctor checked me out, confirmed that my nose was broken, glued my lip back together, and asked me if I wanted some drugs, which I refused. Then he cut a small piece of white athletic tape, which he placed right under my nose on my top lip to hold the flesh together.

It looked ridiculous, and I had to wear it for about a month—this particular injury took a long time to heal. Every time I smiled, that damn cut would open right back up. It made me realize just how much I smile and laugh in my life. Which is so important—maybe the most important. Laughter is a true blessing, one for which I'm truly grateful. Being able to smile and laugh through all

115

the pain and trauma has been one of my greatest lessons and biggest assets.

I have been made fun of for my laugh before. In high school, even the boys I thought were "hot" were always shushing me, my laugh too loud and vibrant for them. There have been times when I've gone to a movie, and afterwards a friend has come up to me and said, "I knew you were in here. There's no one else on earth with that laugh. I could pick you out of a crowd of thousands." I had been embarrassed before about it, not wanting to let it out fully, trying to temper it, trying to quiet it.

After a raucous session of deep laughing, I end up giving out what my friends call the "grandpa" laugh. It's deep and breathy, and for some reason, I always try to talk when I laugh, which makes it even funnier and makes more grandpa sounds. I'm laughing as I write this right now!

I'm so grateful that I fully laugh now—I never hold it back, I lay my head back, open my mouth, and let 'er fly. I just laugh, I've never been a crier—it's something I'm working on—but I laugh so hard I cry at least once a week, if not more. I'm working on that too. I hope to find the space where I laugh every day.

CHAPTER EIGHT:

Life with a Rockstar

The moment I met the love of my life was nothing like a romantic movie scene. I had been cooking in hunting camp for the past couple months, and on this day I got to make the six-hour horseback ride to get supplies for the next little push of hunters. I had a grocery and wish list of supplies needed for all the guys in camp. That list consisted mostly of Copenhagen chewing tobacco, candy bars, and many other addictive items that, if you run out of them on the mountain, will impact your ability to cope with any situation.

In our sleepy little town, there is a small Exxon gas station where you can find all the local novelties, ice cream, and the world's largest jackelope. This funky little store is the cheapest place to buy chew, that disgusting delight most cowboys (and some girls) use to quench their nicotine cravings. I have never liked chew. I tried it a couple times, but I get queasy real quick, and nothing gets you queasier than your first chew. Assuming you

117

can make it past your first dip without passing out and barfing, you're more than likely going to be its next life-long victim.

I had my arms full of several rolls of Copenhagen and a couple bags of Levi Garret. There, towering at the check-out counter, was a big, tall, blue-eyed, smiley cowboy. I'd seen him before in my shenanigans around town—at the square dances, and once at a restaurant when I was there with my previous boyfriend. I had been sitting in a booth across the room from a booth full of young, laughing fellas, and sitting on the end was that tall, smiley cowboy. There I was, supposedly happy with my then-fiancé and mulling over the soup du jour, when that big smile caught my eye. WOW. Zing, tingles, sparks, all the clichés you've ever heard. Even though I had seen him several times over the years, he had never once spoke to me or really even made eye contact. I'd assumed he was either an asshole or was completely uninterested in me. But that smile! It was as if I were coming home. My heart pulled hard, and I remember thinking, "Wow, if that dude ever asked me out I would dump this guy quicker than a moth to a flame." But still no eye contact, still no glances, so I figured my chances were few.

I hadn't thought about him for quite some time. After the break-up with my boyfriend/fiancé that happened shortly after my court case, I had been in a deep depression, a cloudy fog, and had been hiding away at the ranch. Now, as fate would have it, I was crawling out of the mountains, ripe, dirty, and oblivious, and here I was now in a deadlock gaze with those incredible eyes and bright smile. Me with a year's worth of chew in my arms.

He spoke. "Don't ya know that stuff will rot your teeth?"

"Hahahahaaaaaha," I responded awkwardly. "It's not for me."

"Sure," he laughed back as he slipped out the door into the cold October day.

Agghhh, he talked to me! I didn't even think to get his name, or how to find him. Dammit, was it going to be another five years until he spoke to me again?

I was totally twitterpated. A new spark of life had ignited in me, another glimmer of goodness and hope. He was different than the other cowboys I knew. I could sense the kindness exuding from him when he spoke, his gentle manner was almost angelic. There was a lightness that surrounded him in his eyes, his smile. It felt like the universe had sent me an angel, a lifeline saying, "Here is hope. Have faith, because here is an angel."

I rode back into camp the next day dreaming of that smiley, tall cowboy and reliving our meet cute. It was exciting to dream a little dream about who he was, his name, where he was from. He kept my mind busy for the next couple of weeks in hunting camp.

This might have been the first time I was really excited to get out of the mountains. I usually loved this escape from real life amongst the rutting, whistling elk, hungry grizzly bears, and the slow passage of fall to winter. But now I had a quest, an adventure, to track down, this little piece of heaven I had met.

The weeks passed slowly, but finally it was the day to pack up camp and head back to the ranch. I couldn't pack quickly enough. It was Halloween, and I knew we were all going to go into town to join in the festivities. I was hoping this was going to be my chance to see my cowboy again.

I was 20 years old at this time, but the best Halloween parties were at the local watering hole, The Rustic Pine Tavern. I was too young to be at the bar, but this was a time before the crackdown on carding had hit rural Wyoming, and I looked older than I was. The Rustic Pine claims to be the world's most unique bar, and honestly, it might be. The patrons sure are.

I searched the barroom that night looking for my dream cowboy, but couldn't find him. My friends and I had spent the evening hanging out, playing pool, and dancing as much as my little legs would allow. I was heading for the door when a different young man caught me just outside and asked if I'd like to go out. I wasn't interested until I noticed that my cowboy was outside by this time too, and his friend was the one asking me out. I said yes to the date under the condition that he bring his friends and I would bring mine, so it would be more of a group date. That sealed the deal. I saw my cowboy's eyes light up, and his grin got bigger. This would finally be our chance.

Friday, the day of our group date, seemed like an eternity away. I had yet to see if any friends could come with me, and by the time Friday morning came around, only my little sister Savanna was available to join us. On that cool November evening, Savanna and I drove into Jackson to meet our dates.

A gas-guzzling Suburban with County 10 Wyoming plates rolled into the parking lot and slid into a spot beside us. Out came seven fresh young men; Savanna and I were apparently going on a group date with seven guys. The larger responsibility fell to her, since I was only interested in keeping one of those boys' attention.

It's amazing the glimmer of hope that another person can bring to life. I had been damaged goods, heartbroken and kicked to the curb, but the very thought of this sparkly human gave me inspiration and the will to try again. His name was Rocky. I was cautious about falling in love with him, but it happened so fast that I couldn't help myself. He was so honest, funny, vulnerable, and yet also sure of himself. He was the quiet one. But when he spoke, everyone listened.

I thought the name Rocky was so funny for a young man. It was his given name—but he'd been named for his dad's nickname. His friends called him all sort of things—Pile, Rock—and his family called him Rocky T (for his middle name Thomas). The name Rocky is from the ancient Germanic name Rocco, derived from the word hrok, meaning "rest." Rocco was the name of a 14th-century saint who nursed victims of the plague. He is the patron saint of healing the sick.

I didn't actually know the meaning of Rocky's name until I was doing research for this book. But nevertheless, he was a saint to me. My soul was broken, and just when I needed him, he arrived, my saint, my angel. Thus began

121

my love-healing journey. A saint and a cowgirl, or was it a cowboy and a super nova? Actually it was a young, naive, loving, kind man and a broken, beaten down, but hopeful girl believing that life together was light years better than any life spent apart.

I asked him to drive home with me to Dubois that night. We talked, we laughed, and I scared him with my winter driving skills (which are par to none). He made me laugh, a lot, in a subtle way under his breath, with wit I've never heard from a cowboy. At first I didn't believe his gentleness and honesty. It had to be fake. My trust levels were completely annihilated. Was this guy real? Could someone truly be this genuine? I hadn't laughed like that in so long. Laughter felt good welling up inside me, then bursting out. The first time I held his hand, it was shaking terribly, and that was the sweetest thing ever. That made me laugh too, not at him but with him. A gentle giant was sent to me. I could fall into him forever and I did, over time. I was like an abused colt—skittish, flighty, distrustful, and hard to handle.

We were the perfect match. He had the patience and time to give me my space, and he loved me hard, unwavering and honestly. Finally, after all the hard falls I'd taken, this new chapter of my life began with a safe place to land.

Music had always been an integral part of my life, but at the beginning of my twenties, things really took off for my sisters and me. Over the years, in between school and ranching and the theatre, we'd travelled the US and even around the world, singing at country and regional fairs, any place where people appreciated the sound of four-part harmony country music. As word about us had spread, we'd had the opportunity to open for Terri Clark, The Nitty Gritty Dirt Band, and other big names. We'd even gone to Oklahoma City after the bombing and opened for Reba McEntire at the fundraising dinner for the hospital there.

My father hoped we'd go big-time. Through the relationships my parents had cultivated at the theatre and the ranch, they had some opportunities and connections for us all over the country, specifically Los Angeles, New York, and Nashville. With their help, we self-produced a music video filmed at a well-known cowboy bar and a friend's Moosehead Ranch in Moose, Wyoming. Even though social media was barely a thing at the time—MySpace was about the only game in town—we got some good publicity from that music video, and we signed our first big contract with a record company out of Florida called Big Three Productions. They were in the process of merging with DreamWorks Records, Nashville. It was an exciting, eye-opening time in my life, and it should have been my dream come true. But as it happened, by the time it happened, my real dreams were taking shape back in Wyoming.

Rock and I started dating in those years I was back and forth between home and Nashville.

I would say, "Rock, we might have to break up because we might hit it big, and I don't want to have to be tethered. You're in Wyoming, and I'm traveling around the world."

123

This kind of talk always devastated him. It wasn't even precisely true on my end—I was just so afraid to let him love me that whenever I saw a break in the fence, like a flighty colt in a round pen, I felt like I might just run away forever. He always loved me through it, always saying we would make it, always the rock and safe place for me to rest.

Drugs, Sex, Rock 'n' Roll

When I was 21, my sister Vanessa, who'd been living in LA, connected with a British record producer, who offered us a development deal. Rachael, Savanna, and I gathered our sassiest showgirl gear and picked up Vanessa in LA From there, we flew to London for our contract.

We thought for sure this was the break we'd been looking for. The first night we arrived, we had dinner and then walked around enjoying the hype of the big city. I remember we spent some time in popular and touristy Leicester Square. I had Rachael's and my passports in a little purse around my neck. This was just after 9/11, and traveling abroad felt newly sketchy. Heightened security and fear were everywhere.

When we got back to the little flat where we were staying, I realized that our passports had been stolen. First night out the gate. Was this a sign of how this trip was going to go? Undaunted, we met with the producer the next day. He was a flamboyant man around 55 who looked and sounded a lot like Billy Mack, the crazy singer played by Bill Nighy in Love, Actually. At his direction, we cut a few tracks with an up-and-coming younger producer.

It was a totally different genre than we were used to singing. They wanted to present us with an R & B/pop vibe, not unlike an American version of The Spice Girls, and it was a total 180 from the country western music we were used to singing. The schedule was also the opposite of what we were used to. We would go into the studio around 5 or 6 in the evening and record and work until the wee hours of the morning. Ughhh, I hated that. It didn't help that the engineer, the producer, and the songwriter they were using would smoke weed in the studio the entire time—another whole new experience for us.

We lived in London for about six weeks. We were going to miss Thanksgiving in the US, so our producer decided to give us a Thanksgiving UK-style. He invited us out of the city to the small town where he'd been born and raised—and where, honestly, I think he was still living with his mother. By this time I'd become suspicious of the validity of this man and his ability to actually get us anywhere in show business, but when you've been working for a deal most of your life, you turn a blind eye to the questionable. At least, we did.

What was supposed to be a nice Thanksgiving dinner turned quickly into a drug-addled nightmare. Now, I'm all for an awesome unicorn party, but the drug situation was getting intense. I herded my sisters to the apartment upstairs, where we had a hurried discussion, then came back down to confront our producer. During the ensuing conversation, he asked me for some cash to buy some "Coke." I was totally hooked on soda at the time, so I handed him a hundred dollar bill, the only cash I had at the time, and asked him to pick me up "some Diet" and bring me back the change. He gave me a weird look and then left with his entourage of young men. We didn't see him the rest of the weekend.

On the train back into the city, I realized that he had been going to buy real coke, as in cocaine. Wow, I was super naïve—and that is super funny to me now. I can only imagine what he was thinking when I asked for him to bring back the diet and my change. We were always on the fringes of the sex, drugs, and rock 'n roll life, but never took part. It was an energy that never really settled well for me. I didn't want to be a part of that world.

We ended up firing the producer and working solely with the engineer and the songwriter, which went much more smoothly. We ended up cutting three tracks, one of which was on the top

10 Euro charts that year. It was fun and exciting, but we didn't see a dime from that collaboration. We went home full of life experiences but bummed with the reality that a lot of artists experience when trying to break into the music business: scams, misleading contracts, and misguided, eager young artists.

About a year after our London record deal, we were offered another one, a huge one that came in a contract over 200 pages long from a company in Florida. This looked a lot more promising. I remember specifically sitting in the front room at the ranch going through the contract with Dad. I had no idea what all the legal jargon meant and asked Dad about it.

"Does it really matter?" he said. "You'll at least have a record deal. I'd sign it."

All of us sisters were at different places in life. I was working the ranch, Vanessa was in LA still working towards an acting career, Savanna was attending Belmont University in Nashville, and Rachael had just graduated from Jackson Hole High School. I was very hesitant to sign the deal, especially since I was the only one of our group who wrote songs. I didn't want to be stuck in a publishing deal forever. But Dad was convincing.

We didn't know then that just because you get a contract, it doesn't mean you should take it. Definitely take the time and money to have an entertainment attorney look over all contracts, and go into negotiations knowing that you are the asset! Don't go in thinking that the record company is doing you any favors. At any rate, we all signed the contract, and within weeks we were off on our way to St. Petersburg, Florida.

Once again, it was a very exciting time and a ride to new heights, new dreams. This time was markedly different from our ragged arrival in London. Here, we had two Mustang convertibles that were all ours to drive around. Our home for the duration of the contract was a beautiful cedar townhome whose back door opened right onto the sandy beach. We had our own swimming pool. Life was easy and high on the hog.

We were shuttled back and forth on a private jet to and from Nashville. The best day was when we were set to record with one of the biggest producers in the business, James Stroud, who produced many big artists such as Tracey Lawrence, Daryl Singletary, and Clay Walker, just to name a few. He was the real deal and a big deal.

We walked into the studio for our session, and there on the studio roster of folks who had been recording that day were the names of Willie Nelson, Toby Keith, and Brad Paisley. I remember brushing my hand over the list of humans in complete disbelief that there, right below those names in black, bold print, was The Saddle Rock Sisters, our band name. I was completely humbled and star struck. That was a magical day.

We recorded a three-song album. The tracks were all very fun and catchy but looking back, they lacked the honesty, depth, and integrity to make a great hit. Back then, though, we thought we were on the cusp of great things. But those songs never really took off. We didn't go back into the studio for several months after that.

Thanksgiving came around, and this time we were flown on a private jet to the Bahamas, where the company had rented out the famous Bridge Suite, suspended 16 stories off the ground between the two towers of the Atlantis hotel. We had our own butler, and things were very bougie.

It was all a great distraction, which was maybe part of the point. I started feeling that things weren't going to transpire the way we had hoped. There was something missing. They weren't allowing us to record our own songs, and we weren't being called into the studio much anymore. I was so used to being busy and working hard that the downtime in between studio sessions made me anxious and bored. I wanted to be in full push mode, getting things done.

What I didn't realize was that my sister was having a weird relationship with a man high up in the company, and he was holding her professionally and emotionally hostage when she refused to have sex with him. She wasn't really even sharing with the rest of us what was going on, I believe in fear that we would judge her, and also because she felt that she had an obligation to us to keep quiet and keep this guy happy for the sake of our future success.

It's an all-too-familiar situation for women in the entertainment industry. It was truly depressing and horribly wrong on all levels, what this man was getting away with. Once I found out what was happening, I couldn't bear to see him or speak with him. I felt horrible for my sister, horrible that she felt so much responsibility to all of us and that she so didn't want to screw up our careers that she felt she had to have this relationship with him.

Things started to slowly unravel. Our Mustangs were taken away and replaced by a single, more economical vehicle. Our salary was dramatically cut. We were never called into the studio anymore, and I was really feeling like we'd been forgotten. It was painful to be there with nothing to do, while the dream of what could have been slowly slid down the drain.

We sought legal counsel, but after reading our contracts the lawyers said we didn't really have much choice except to let the contract run out. Unfortunately, I had a publishing contract with my songs that kept me tied to them for another 15 years. Another life lesson notch on the belt.

Rachael and Vanessa decided that they'd had enough of the singing group. Savanna and I still wanted to continue. We came back home to Wyoming discouraged, but determined to still try. It was heartbreaking to face all the people at home. We didn't want to explain, so we didn't really know what to say. "Things didn't work out. There was a bigger plan for us all."

Savanna and I continued to perform all over. We produced another three-song demo, got some more notice, and then went back to Nashville and participated in a new television series that was called Can You Duet, a televised competition in which we placed in the top 20. At that point, Savanna had just had enough and wanted to pursue her acting career, and I ended up as a solo act.

It was very hard for me to learn how to perform alone after 15 years of performing with my sisters. I felt naked without them, but I couldn't turn off the music inside. Music had been my healing, and my songs have been my through line.

Rocky and Me

By this point, Rocky and I had dated for so many years that my father began to ask him, "When you two kids getting hitched?" My dad would school me: "Now, honey, why would he buy the cow when he can get the milk for free?" It sounds like archaic, misogynistic talk, but that's what my dad felt—especially as someone coming from the LDS religion, where most people who date for a year get engaged within that year, and then married. Rock and I dated for six years. Even though I was flighty, the guilt of not being married was severe, and the idea of "living in sin" for that long was foundationally wrong to me. But Rock was of a different culture, and he wasn't ready.

Rock went to Utah for a while, where he got a job with a famous horse trainer. I was so excited for him and thought this was the break he'd been looking for. I was still in Nashville doing the singing gig, and this was Rock's first time away from home. He had grown up on a cattle ranch on the Shoshone Indian reservation in Crowheart, Wyoming, his father a direct descendant of Chief Washakie of the eastern Shoshone tribe.

Life usually looks like that for most cattle ranchers' kids or natives there. Most of them do a small stint in college, rodeo a little, or maybe get a basketball scholarship, but they always come back to the ranch eventually and stay there, raising their families and living out the rest of their lives on the same ranch they grew up on.

Now, there is nothing wrong with that. Hell, that is how I was raised too, thinking one day I would run my family's ranch. But life can be smothering there for someone who wants to branch out, reach high, and try something new. It's almost as if the people left behind feel a little resentment or anxiety, which puts lot of strain on the ones leaving—especially on the reservation. I feel there is a generational trauma that has been passed down from traumatic Indian wars and displacement, and it's deeply rooted spiritually and even subconsciously. It seems as if they have to stick together because that is the only way they will still survive.

I understood this because that is similar to what I felt with my seven siblings. But this way of thinking and believing is too heavy for the person soaring. They cannot take everyone with them. The drag is too heavy, and at some point, you have to let go of the ties behind to really soar.

Rock wasn't ready to soar. He still had much responsibility at home. His father had been ill with cancer, again. He was diagnosed the first time when Rock was five, then had recurring bouts with it since. Rocky felt an obligation to be there for him. I was disappointed. I wanted big things for Rock, so I pushed him. I pushed him just as hard as I pushed myself, with the same persistence and grit that it took me to walk again. But he is not like me. He is slow and methodical, and he takes his time. I'm fast, reactive, quick-triggered, and forceful.

Rock's history of trauma with his father's cancer and the sense of responsibility he felt toward his family and home were among the things that bound us, as different as we were. We'd both had larger-than-life experiences despite our youth, and we'd both been hugely responsible to our families. But he left that job with the famous horse trainer and went back home. His decision left me thinking he wasn't going to change or be able to move past his familial ties, and, in a way, I was right. His father did need him.

We broke up for a time after all this. I told him that he needed to find out what he really wanted in his life and how he was going to make that happen. I didn't know then that he wanted me for his life, that this what mattered to him. He would say to me, "I love you and want to be with you," but I didn't know how to receive it. I was so afraid of being someone's world. I couldn't accept that. Way too much responsibility for an effed-up human barely figuring how to walk again, barely knowing who I was amidst a crazy world of fame, fortune, and music. I was such a fool. Here I had the greatest gift of true love standing beside me and waiting there for me to accept his loving arm to lean on, but I was too damaged, too scared, and too proud to see it.

During our break-up, my best girlfriend of 15 years and I decided to take a trip to Mexico. We flew into Cancun and drove to the border of Belize, enjoying our way. We spent a couple weeks leisurely enjoying Tulum and Playa del Carmen, with their beautiful beaches of pure white sand.

I had taken Spanish in college and high school, and I still had enough fluency that we moved easily through the country.

As we were coming to the end of our trip, I rose very early one morning, walked down to the beach, sat, and meditated. Sitting on the sand, eyes closed, the ocean's breath heavy in my ears and a gentle, salty breeze encompassing me, I heard a voice as loud as day say, "You are to go home and marry Rocky O'Neal. Everything you've been telling yourself is a lie. Do this."

It scared me at first. I jumped up and looked around. I was still by myself—not a soul in sight and yet, that's exactly what it was, a soul, even if I couldn't see it. Trembling, I sank back onto the sand and closed my eyes.

133

"Go home and marry Rocky O'Neal. This is your destiny."

I was again shaken to my core. The voice was not a whisper, but instead loud and commanding in my ears. I knew this voice. I had heard it before, but not in this manner or tone. Was this the voice of spirit? My higher self? God? Jesus? The Holy Ghost? All the words felt right. Rocky was my destiny, so why was I trying to run away from him? Did I believe I was worthy of such love? Too afraid to have something go good in my life after so much heartbreak and trauma? Terrified to step into glory?

In the end, I was more afraid to not fulfill my destiny. Never had anything in my life been so clearly laid out before me. I couldn't get home quick enough. I called Rock and asked him to meet me in Jackson. I apologized, prayed for his forgiveness, and told him what I had experienced in Mexico, about the voice that I had heard, that he was my destiny, and that I was so sorry for not being able to let go of my huge heart wall that I had built up over years of abuse, mistrust, and pain. That heart wall was so thick, heavy, and hidden that only time, attention, and love were going to bring it down.

It was not an easy task for either Rock or I to manage, but together, we could move mountains. There is a beautiful quote from William Shakespeare's Midsummer Night's Dream that says, "The course of true love never did run smooth." So began our true love adventure, some years spent soaring high above the proverbial peaks, then years barely trudging through darkest, low valleys, dreaming for days of smooth, easy-riding trails.

Rocky asked me to marry him in September of that year when we were both 25. It was a very simple, beautiful, honest proposal. He packed a picnic lunch of our favorite sandwiches, snacks, and, of course, the finest dark chocolate, and drove me up a winding, bumpy dirt road toward the base of Ramshorn Peak. The truck rolled to a stop near a small patch of quaking aspens vibrating with an array of changing colors from deep green to fiery peach and then to orange. A dream picture of mountains surrounding a forest floor scattered with divine colors, the Wyoming wind talking through the quaking leaves. Rocky took my hand. As he knelt down, I couldn't even look at him. His hand was shaking in that sweet, loving way it did when we first met, and then the most beautiful words slipped from his quivering voice: "I love you, Jess, will you marry me?"

There in his big, strong hand was a beautiful turquoise and diamond ring, the most unique ring I had ever seen. Crying, I said, "Of course! I love you!" We kissed in this incredible setting, holding each other tight. This moment, I was living my destiny. Rock carved our names in the biggest quaky (aspen tree) he could find: Rock + Jess = True Love. Our names carved into time for generations, proclaiming our love amongst all creation. I often wonder if, years from now a hiker or hunter will come across our little love grove and wonder who Rock and Jess are. If they are still the equivalent of true love.

I chose my destiny, and his name is Rocky. When I need a gentle reminder, I can head to those trees to see our names etched deep in the dark black of the tree, its trunk morphed and stretched from years of growth, hard winters, and exposure. I'll reread the words of this book and know we chose each other. Some would say that true love does not grow on trees, but I know our true love is tied to the quakies. We proclaimed it as deep-rooted, grown together toward Mother Earth's womb, blooming with seasons, retreating during cold times, always growing, always changing. Bound together with the element of turquoise of my ring, aiding us with trust, spiritual development, devotion, and uniqueness. Rock + Jess = True Love.

Cowboy Living

Our first years of marriage weren't that different from our dating years. I was still travelling, singing, doing shows, and working at the ranch. Three weeks after our wedding, we started a fencing company in the middle of January in Crowheart, Wyoming. Not fencing like dueling with skinny swords fencing, but the work-your-ass-off tamping, digging, shoveling, and what I like to call receiving your PhD (post hole digger degree) kind of fencing. Honest, hard ass labor.

If you haven't been to Crowheart in January, let me paint a picture for you. Wind: the natural movement of air of any velocity, but wind in Crowheart is of extreme velocity and ranks number one in the US, with an annual average speed of 12.9 mph. It takes a tough human to be able withstand the winter winds. Learning how to move amongst it, instead of against it. We were inspired, excited, motivated. We felt like we were crushing adulthood—mind you, we lived in a 1970s-vintage shitty trailer on the

Wind River Indian reservation—not vintage in a stylish way, but rather bachelor ranch hands who've lived there for two decades kind of way: three-inch, pale green shag carpet, "running" water that was more like a trickle, and a wood stove as the only heat source.

During those early years, it like I was living the lyrics to the Garth Brooks song "Whatcha Gonna Do with a Cowboy." (Please tell me some Garth Brooks fans are reading this—even better if you are reading this, Garth, you are my hero, and Chris LeDoux was my first love when you did this song together!)

You can see it takes a special kinda woman
To put up with the life a cowboy leads
'Cause his boots are always muddy
And his beer drinkin' buddies
They'll camp out on your couch and never leave
Don't even start to think you're gonna change him
You'd be better off to try and rope the wind
What he see is what he's got
And he can't be what he's not
And honey you can't hide him from your friends
'Cause what'cha gonna do with a cowboy
When that old rooster crows at dawn
When he's lyin' there instead of getttin' out of bed
And puttin' on his boots and gettin' gone
What you gonna do when he says
     honey I've got half a mind to stay
What'cha gonna do with a cowboy
When he don't saddle up and ride away

What'cha gonna do with a cowboy
When he don't saddle up and ride away

~ "Whatcha Gonna Do with a Cowboy,"
by Garth Brooks and Mark D. Sanders

During those trailer years, our friend lived with us. After one fun-filled night at the local watering hole, the three of us made the long trek home from Dubois to Crowheart with our cousin. Me and the cowboys. Yes, it smelled exactly like you would imagine. We were all sleeping in the front room that night, as it was the only room with any heat, albeit from a wood stove. If you have any experience with men sleeping after a night of heavy beer drinking, you probably already know that the snore volume goes from a small hum to the equivalent of a military jet trying to break the sound barrier. It gets a little out of hand. I was trying to sleep peacefully amidst the symphonic bass that was shaking the trailer. Three men, three different snores, and none of them in similar rhythm. No number or combination of pillows and covers could effectively muffle or mute the noise.

This had to stop. I resorted to stealth. Slinking from the bed and army crawling to the couch where my friend was sleeping, I waited for his next exhale, reached up to his face, brushed past his bushy 1970s porn star stache, and, ever so gently, plugged his nose. I held my fingers there, light but steady, hoping to God he didn't wake up. What would I say? "Uhhhhhhhh, just hanging out down here on the floor, pluggin' your nose..."

He tried to breathe three times, and then stirred. I shot down to the floor as flat as I could. There was some huffing, then he finally rolled over onto his side. Mission one complete. I army-crawled once again to the other couch, where victim number two lay sleeping and snoring loud enough to call in the wolves. Slowly, like a sloth, I once again lay flat as I could to the floor and snaked my arm up and over the couch cushions. I could feel Britt's hot breath in my hand—not just on it, but literally in it. I knew I was close to his nose so I went in for the clamp—but he moved, so I shot back down again. I waited until he started snoring again, and then I went in for the kill, plugging his nose until his breath—and the snoring—stopped, and he became uncomfortable enough to roll over.

I was actually trying hard to not laugh as I pictured the scene in my head: me creeping around on the floor plugging noses. But a girl's gotta do what a girl's gotta do, especially when it comes to sleep.

Then there was one: the last snorer, my hubby. I crawled back into bed next to my main squeeze, spooned right up to him, and then swooped my arm around, pinching off his nostrils with my fingers. He gasped for breath, and I flung myself in the opposite direction.

We lay quietly. What was this? No snores? Ahhh. Just as I was closing my eyes, even more exhausted after my shenanigans, the sound of a chain saw started up from the corner of the room. Our friend was back at it with more fervor than before. Then, as if cued by a conductor, Britt entered, softly at first, but with a triumphant finish.

Back to the floor, I went, crawling around, pinching nostrils, and seeking sanity. The fun and games continued for the rest of that whole night. I wish now that cell phones with good cameras had been a thing back then, because that would surely have been a YouTube sensation.

I still use this tactic to this day. It is a sure way to make someone stop snoring. You're welcome. The moral of the story? You can pinch your friends, you can pinch your nose, and I can pinch my friends' noses.

We had many good years together in that humble trailer. Dreaming of our future ahead, we both worked tirelessly toward our dreams, growing and changing—sometimes together, sometimes apart. Our trails always came back to each other no matter what we did or where life took us. Little did we know that our greatest uphill climb was just beginning.

CHAPTER NINE:

Daddy Issues

During the summer season before my 27th birthday, I had been playing the lead role in a musical *Seven Brides for Seven Brothers* at my family's theatre. The season was coming to the end. The quaking aspens were starting their yearly transformation from healthy green to pale yellow into bright yellow to vibrant peach, settling into a red and then dying off finally at crisp brown. September was usually my favorite month, but since my accident autumn brought an underlying melancholy for me. The show had been running since May 28, so the end of the season couldn't come fast enough for me. I had been working nights at the theater and days at the ranch, saddling, riding horses, and dancing for 17 hours a day, six days a week. I was exhausted.

The day after the last performance, I was to ride six hours to our hunting camp, where I planned to read, write, ride my horse, and be in nature with some of my favorite people on Earth: Rock, my dad, and my sisters

Savanna and Vanessa. That Wednesday night, I was especially tired. I hadn't slept well in two days, and I felt an unsettling, uneasy anxiety. During those sleepless nights I'd been watching movies to try to get to sleep and keep my mind occupied: *We Are Marshall, Pan's Labyrinth, Lake House*—all movies about death. Looking back, it's clear to me that this was a nudge from the universe, another little hint saying, "Listen, get quiet. Things are shifting." The unease had consumed me for the better part of a week. I was having trouble eating.

I'd had this feeling before, and I was fearful of what it might mean. A deep sense of loss was washing over me, and I was anxious that I was going to lose someone. At the time, I thought it was my husband. He was guiding hunters up in the mountains with no cell service and no way to contact him. All I wanted was to feel his incredibly strong arms around me, holding me through this weird time and not letting me go.

I had been meditating, praying, doing yoga, and all the other "right" things, trying to relieve this constant worry. Thursday afternoon, just a couple of hours before the show was about to begin, I knew that if I didn't get some rest, there was no way I was going to make it through the 90-minute performance. Completely exhausted, I lay my head down. I had just drifted off to sleep when my cell phone rang. I shot out of bed, and there on the screen was Rocky's name. There is no cell service in camp or anywhere nearby, so I knew that either he was somehow out of the mountains or that something was wrong. I was so shocked, I answered it by saying, "Honey, are you okay?"

He replied, "Yes, are you?"

"Yes, I'm totally fine. Why?"

"You don't know?"

"Don't know what?"

"They didn't tell you?"

"Who? Didn't tell me what?"

Rocky sighed. There was a long pause. His voice, when it came, was shaky. "Honey…your dad had a heart attack and he…he died."

I lost control of my limbs and crumbled to the floor. The phone felt like it weighed 100 pounds, and I could barely keep my hand around it. My entire body felt like it was in drying concrete. I slowly crawled out of my room, tripping over my sluggish legs and trying to stand up and walk into the living room, where some of my friends were passing time until the show started.

Rocky's voice was in my ear. "Jess, are you okay?"

My friends were talking. "What happened, Jess?" "Are you okay?" Four voices all speaking to me at once.

Pulling myself up in the doorway, gasping hard to get the words out: "Rocky, are you sure?"

"Yes, I was there."

"Are you really sure?

"Yes, honey, when I got to him, he was gone."

"What happened?"

"I think he had a heart attack while guiding his hunter."

My legs gave out again. I could not gain control of them. I was telling them, "Get up, you bastards, and walk," but they would not work. I lay heaped in a quivering pile, not crying, but shaking, with no strength left in my body at all.

"Where is he?" I asked.

"I'm sure they took him to the morgue."

I'd never really heard that word in everyday conversation, let alone felt it like a lightning bolt through my soul. As soon as he said "morgue," a numbing pang bolted through every cell, vein, and joint of my body.

"What happens now? What do I do, Rocky?"

"Honey, I'll be there soon."

From the theatre downstairs, I could hear the usual western theme songs, slightly muffled but still clearly audible, and the bustle of show goers excited for the performance. I knew that I had to conjure up the strength to find my mother and other siblings who were below me, working, and give them the kind of news you dread hearing your whole life.

The stairs on the building's exterior had never seemed steeper. My legs felt like I'd just run a marathon. Each step felt like it was miles long. I crept down, sliding and hugging the side of the building all the way to the bottom. As I reached the last step, a vehicle pulled up with my youngest siblings, 10-year-old Cheyenne and 12-year-old Golden, inside. I stumbled to the driver's side window. At the wheel was a parent of one of their friends, someone I'd never met. I stammered for words. I choked out in a low breathless whisper, "Please take them away from here and come back in an hour. I'm sorry, please, I'll explain later." The man could clearly sense the urgency in my voice, and he drove away.

144

Although there were only about 100 yards from the alley to the front door of the theatre, I needed every ounce of my being and strength to cross them. As I entered the building, I saw my beautiful mother at the ticket booth, helping guests and smiling. My legs started shaking violently now over the daunting task before me.

"Mom, I need to talk to you. Come into the office, please."

She paled as her smile dwindled.

"Why?"

"Please, Mom, come with me."

"No, tell me now."

"Mom, please, please just come with me."

She knew something huge was coming. She could see the pain in my eyes and sense my desperation emitting sheer loss.

"Jessica, stop it. You can tell me right here. I'm not going."

"Please, Mom."

"No."

I took a breath. "Mom, Dad had a heart attack guiding his hunter," I began, adding, almost under my breath, "he's gone."

She began hitting me repeatedly and yelling, "No, no, he's not! You don't know! Where is he?"

My sister Savanna walked in on the scene.

"What's going on?"

I turned to my sister. "Vanna, Dad had a heart attack and he…he died." That word hurt so badly to say that it made me sick to my core to let it out of my mouth.

She crumpled to the couch in disbelief, wailing, "No, no! Are you sure?"

Mother was walking around, crazed, yelling, crying, hitting. "Where is he? I want to see him!"

"Mom, he's at the...(I mustered up the strength to get the nasty word out of my mouth...out of my body) morgue."

"No, no, he's not!" Mom ran out the door to her car. I managed to get the front passenger door open in time to hop in as she sped away.

"Mom, where are you going?" By this time, I could feel the physical effects of shock wearing off a bit. I wasn't shaking as hard, now that I knew I had to be strong.

"I'm going to the hospital," Mom insisted.

"He's not there."

"How do you know?"

"They said they were taking him to the morgue."

We screeched to a stop at the front entrance of the emergency room. Leaving the car idling,

Mom leapt from the vehicle. I couldn't keep up with her. My legs, ughhhh, my legs...

"Where is my husband, Cameron Garnick?" Mom was quivering while speaking to the receptionist at the front desk. "Where is he? I want to see him."

What unfolded played out like every hospital scene in the movies, with people bustling about, my mom yelling, friends showing up, people asking questions that had no answers, and no one making eye contact.

Then the big, heavy wooden doors labeled "Emergency Entrance, Personnel Only" swung open, and out stepped a young, fresh, lean doctor. I could tell by his demeanor that he had prepared a quick speech as he'd walked down the long corridor to us. "Are you Mrs. Garnick?" he asked the woman who was obviously the most hysterical person in the room. "Would you come with me?'

Mom refused. "Where is my husband Cameron? I want to see him!"

"Ma'am, step out with me."

"No!" she said, more stern than ever. "Where is my husband?"

Finally, in a little room just off of the lobby of the emergency room, the doctor told the story once again—the story that was becoming my story, the invitation to the club you never want to be a part of: the "My Dad Died" club. Heart attack something something, guiding hunters, something something, I'm so sorry. So many words, but all I heard was gone, dead, morgue. I was shaking again, my legs unsteady and numb, losing control.

The rest of the day was a blur. I felt deeply that I had to be the one to tell my other eight siblings. I had a daunting job. I called my brother Sky, who was a senior in high school at the time, and told him to meet me at the fabric store across from the morgue. He now had my two youngest siblings, Cheyenne and Golden, with him. I had to call a friend in New York City to go find my brother Creed, who was at school at Juilliard in New York City. I found my sister Vanessa in an airport, where she was between flights from Panama to Wyoming. I called my sister living in Florida.

147

Was that all of them? Yes.

When we finally got to Daddy, we found him lying on a metal slab in the chapel/viewing room of the morgue. The shiny, harsh metal slab is still vivid in my mind. It looked so cold, rigid, and uncomfortable. But Dad looked peaceful. I had never seen him so still—he was not a calm human, always moving, never sitting still, always rocking back and forth. He was fiery, vibrant, even scary at times. Peaceful was not a word I would use to describe him.

The stillness and silence was alarming. The hush in the room was heavy, with only whimpers and sniffles echoing off the high walls. Waves of moaning, crying, yelling, and every vocalization of grief surrounded him. His red wool shirt had a flattened roll of toilet paper tucked into his front left pocket. (He always carried extra toilet paper like this, and it's one of the things I miss about him. He was always prepared for whatever crap life was giving him.) He had dark-colored Wranglers, dirty from long days in the back country. His clothes smelled of cold morning campfires, old saddles, and his sweet sweat.

I draped over his body, holding his cold, limp hand. As I stared at him, looking for the slightest movement, my mind played tricks on me. I thought I could see his chest rise with a breath, breaking me out of this nightmare.

All eight of us kids, my mother, and my fathers' parents took turns holding him, piling on him as we had in life. We were hoping and praying against all logic that he would wake, but there was never a breath nor a budge, only utter stillness.

The mortician came in periodically to ask if we needed food or water. There was pressure to make decisions: cremation or burial? Which casket? We grieved there with Dad for a couple days, taking naps on the pews if needed, leaving in shifts, having to be reminded to eat. This is the elusiveness of grief: some things are very clear and poignant, while small daily tasks can be completely overlooked—brushing your teeth, eating, showering. Time seems to stop, but life around you is still bustling. Many friends stopped in to share our grief, check on us, and feed us. It is during this heavy fog of grief that friends' and loved ones' support is needed most.

Our family has never done anything the normal way or the "right" way. We've always just done things our way. So when the morgue guy continued to press us—the body was getting stale, there are legalities for how long you can leave a body not embalmed if you are burying— I decided we needed to talk.

My mother, my grandmother, and I were ushered into a small room off the side of the chapel. There, in a cheaply decorated room full of plastic floral arrangements, boxes of tissues, and squeaky chairs, we looked over burial options. It became clear that nothing that they had to offer suited Dad. When we said our thank yous and asked for Dad to be embalmed so we could transport him soon, the mortician was baffled. They had never had anyone refuse service.

When they were done, we called an attorney friend to see what our rights were for transporting the body. We loaded Dad up in the back of the family Ford Excursion and transported him to our theatre. There, we placed Dad center stage surrounded by pictures, saddles, and all his cowboy gear—rope, wooly chaps, leather cuffs, his old hats, anything that reminded us of him on this earth.

It was difficult for me to hold and hug him after the embalmment. He no longer smelled like Dad, he smelled like toxic chemicals, and after touching him, my own skin smelled the same. I needed a solution, because I wasn't done holding him. I tried smudging him with sage and wiping him down with baby wipes. Finally I found one of my favorite essential oils, pine, and rubbed it all over him, masking the scent of chemicals with something that was fundamentally Dad: the forest.

I slept below Dad that day, hidden underneath the gurney and the heavy Hudson Bay blankets that draped over him. No one knew I was there under the table, but I couldn't leave him. Mourners came and went all hours of the day, and at one point there was a line around the block with folks waiting to pay their respects. Lying under the table, hidden, I heard secret wishes to Dad and our family. I heard apologies from bridges burnt; I witnessed grief and mourning in its every stage, from the closest loved ones to mere acquaintances. It gave me an incredible perspective on my father's life.

You see, grief is not something you can prepare for. It is not something that you can have any idea of how you might react. Most of us go through life thinking somehow we are going to defy the odds of ever having to feel grief, but we don't. Somehow, someday, we all succumb to grief's humbling blows. Grief might be similar to death in that it is so completely individual we can never truly tell others how to handle it or what to do or even what to expect. Many of us spend most of our lives running away from, self-medicating from, and avoiding these intense game changers. Pain and grief are divine healing powers, our ultimate teachers, and our truest mirrors.

In the days and weeks that followed my father's passing, my mother couldn't decide where to bury him. In the throes of mourning, we went looking for a gravesite, trying to find the perfect spot to lay my dad down to rest. Dad's death came as such a shock to everyone, and especially my mom. She and Dad did not have life insurance nor a will, and had not thought about where they wanted to be buried. We were all having to face so many things, especially my mother facing her own mortality. It seemed as though we could not find a place to please her.

For a couple of days that felt like two weeks, we drove around the county, and each one of those days we saw a black bear or grizzly in the forest or on the roadside, which is good medicine. It's said that the spirit of the bear is a strong source of support in times of difficulty. It provides courage and a stable foundation to face challenges. When the bear shows up as a spirit guide in your life, it's perhaps time to stand for your beliefs or your truth. The bear is also a guide to take leadership in your life or in other people's lives. Its presence inspires respect. Bear strength and powerful stature will inspire you to step into a leadership role in your life and take action without fear.

I felt my father deeply when those bears were near. It was as if he was guiding us, showing us a path of peace

151

through little reminders that he was close. After much thought and consideration, our friends who lived near my childhood home in Buffalo Valley offered their plot of land to bury Dad until we found a better, permanent resting place for him. They stipulated that we use no heavy machinery or equipment, that we leave the land looking like there was no grave there, and that we move him within 10 years. It was agreed that this would be his "for now" resting place.

My father's funeral was epic. He was an epic man, so he deserved an epic ending here. At our family ranch, there were an estimated 500 humans who came to pay their respects to my dad. We loaded him in his casket on the back of a wagon with a beautiful team of horses hitched to the front. Surrounding the wagon were the men who had been chosen to be the pall bearers, and most of my family preceded him in a horse-drawn surrey with fringe on top, just like it was out of a song in *Oklahoma!*

It was an incredibly beautiful fall day, very warm, and above us, sitting on the wind, was a powerful red tail hawk soaring overhead the entire four-hour service. Each child spoke memories of Dad, as did my mother and grandmother. We sang songs in his honor, mostly cowboy songs and songs from musical theatre shows that he had loved or performed in during his days as an actor. There were many tears—some happy, some sad, and some even mad with the feeling that Dad had departed so young and quickly, so unexpectedly.

For me, it was all a bit of a haze. During this time, I was

pushing so hard to keep myself together for my siblings and for my mother. I had an incredible sense of responsibility to all of them. What would happen now? How would we survive? What would happen with the ranch?

When the time came after the service to dress my father's body in his burial clothes, I gathered with most of my siblings and several of my dad's friends. We carefully handled his heavy, cumbersome body and dressed him. We hammered each nail into the pinewood box lovingly crafted by one of his best friends. We loaded the casket into the back of the Excursion once again, packed as many people as we could in it, then drove his body over to the burial site in Moran, Wyoming.

There was no formal funeral procession. But Dad had driven US Highway 26 every day for 15 years, and the highway department had been working on that road for seven of them. So when we brought Dad over to the ranch for the service, the highway workers, who knew our vehicles, stopped the entire project, came to the side of the road, took off their construction hats, and placed them over their hearts as we passed. It was an incredibly moving, loving gesture during that time of mourning.

The meaning of "six feet under" becomes very visceral when you have to dig that by hand with a spade shovel, using buckets to remove the dirt. It took us five hours of digging and chipping away at the layers and sediments of the earth compacted over thousands of years to create that six- foot by four-foot rectangle. My siblings, my mom, my husband, and Dad's friends all took

153

turns digging Dad's grave. It was an arduous task, yet immensely healing. We took our time. We sang songs, told stories, cried, and were often weak with grief, but we were inspired by the memory of my father to carry on.

It took creativity and every muscle we could muster to slowly lower Dad into the grave without breaking the casket. Then, like something out of an old movie western, there was the snick of the shovel cutting into the pile of loose dirt, and the heave and thump of dirt clods drummed onto the pine coffin. The sounds echoing throughout the dark forest. A hush fell over us as we shoveled then tamped, shoveled then tamped the rich earth packed down around and sealing him back into the mineral and sediment that comprised him. Reverently, we finished by singing his favorite hymn:

Whenever I hear the song of a bird or look at the blue, blue sky,
Whenever I feel the rain on my face or the wind as it rushes by,
Whenever I touch a velvet rose or walk by a lilac tree,
I'm glad that I live in this beautiful world
heavenly father created for me.

~ "My Heavenly Father Loves Me,"
Traditional

With that, we laid our prayers in the dirt: a simple cross made from two sticks at his head, and a bouquet of wildflowers—the only signs that we had been there toiling all day. It was very difficult for me to walk away, but I knew he would enjoy this beautiful resting spot in the wild, ancient, untouched country of Buffalo Valley, laid in peace amongst native people, grizzly trails, and mountain men.

I look back at that time now and see that it was powerful to be able to hold my Dad's body, to be a part of it, to dress him, and to know that it was literally just a shell of a man no longer present. The amazing things about him—his big, beautiful voice; his handsome face; his strong arms and legs; and his charismatic charm—were no longer present. I realized that energy is the only thing connecting us into our bodies. There is a magnetic shift when we leave, like two magnets no longer pushed together but flipped over to opposing sides.

CHAPTER TEN:

The Wake

My brother Sky coined a term perfect for grief: "Don't give a fuckery." In the wake of my father's death, all concerns about the outside world, material items, ego, and insecurities seeped from my thoughts. Only the present mattered. Love is all that remains, whether you are longing for it, losing it, or feeling it.

It began to become clear to me that I had been putting on a show most my life, trying to uphold some standard for others, society, myself, and my family. Grief showed me that all things I had worried about most my life were minute details in the grand scheme of things. I finally gave myself permission to act exactly how I felt. If I wanted to cry, I did. If I needed to laugh, I did. If I didn't want to talk to someone, I wouldn't.

I thought I had been an honest person, but I had still been hiding behind how I might make other people feel or what they were thinking. After my father's death, honesty became my new wings. In my grief, I no longer had the luxury of pretending. Truth was emitting from my very being. Grief shook my world to its core, stripping away all the bullshit that had been covering up my true self. Relationships became deeper and more meaningful. My dreams became bigger, more tangible, and urgent. It took my father's death for me to really live fully. Once again, I had been graced with a do-over, a chance to start anew. Grief saved my life.

In the days after my father's service, we still had guests coming to the ranch, so we went about our business as usual—and by that, I mean that we kept the business going. I didn't sleep or eat much for days, but my daily familiar chores were comforting, or, at the very least, stable. Wake up, feed and water the horses, wrangle the horses from the pasture, and saddle 'em for the morning ride.

One day, we had a couple arriving from New York to stay at the ranch. I went to saddle up my horse, but my body was weak from mourning. No one tells you much about the physical ramifications of grief, about losing your will to eat, drink water, or sleep. It's as if your capacity to thrive dies along with the person.

My saddle felt as if the weight of the world was hung from it. With one final heave and all the force in my body, my beautifully crafted, handmade saddle that my father had given to me on my 15th birthday landed upon the withers of my sweet paint mare. I went totally weak, leaned into my mare, and bawled, even howled. She stood strong and leaned back into me as if saying, "I got you." The sharp smell of leather and horse sweat had never been so comforting. I buried my face hard into her mane and just...let...go.

I felt a quick tap on my shoulder. "Excuse me, we're here for our ride?"

That day's guests had arrived and were ready to head out. In a thick fog, feeling almost robotic, I gave them the riding instruction demo, got them on their horses, and led them out of the arena and due north at a slow, melancholy pace. I was so relieved to be out in front where I could let my tears flow free. I've never been a good crier. I'd spent most of my life trying not to cry, trying to cowboy up to be tough.

We started up the steep trail, one I knew was probably a little too much for the novice riders, but my heart was pulling me to this certain ridge. As we were switchbacking, I noticed a new track in the trail. It was the track of a man, fairly fresh and made since the last rain. Could they be Dad's tracks? They were the same size and from the same boot maker, I got very excited, and my pain eased for a slight moment. It was as if Dad was leading me, leaving little hints in the earth that he was still with me.

We climbed to the top of the ridge and as we crested the butte, a beautiful rainbow beamed from one end of the sky to the other. I turned my horse into the wind. The quick breeze energized me—it was strong, and I felt it might blow me off the mountain and carry me away. At least, that's what I was wishing.

Once again I let go and released the fear of someone seeing me cry, released the pressure of trying to keep it all together. My tears streaked across my face. I had forgotten that I was with guests. A man rode up beside me and put his hand on my leg. "Miss, are you alright?"

I shot back into reality. "No, I'm not. My father passed away a few days ago. I'm sorry, I'm feeling very emotional."

There was some conversation about how sorry they were, how they wished they had known. They asked if they should stay at the ranch or leave. It was all a little blurry, but telling the truth and not having to put on a show for them felt very good. I was releasing.

We ended up staying on the mountain for a long while. They asked questions about Dad and our family, and it felt good to answer them. I could have stayed forever, but I realized it was way past lunch, and what was supposed to have been an hour ride had turned into four.

I turned my mare down the steep embankment, and we bushwhacked our way back to the ranch. Not once did the guests complain, even though I was taking them down some very steep game trails that made even my butt pucker as I looked at the straight plunge down the mountainside to the land below. Not once did this sweet, older, out-of-shape couple who hadn't ridden in 30 years even flinch at what I was asking of them. We had an adventure, a moment of true vulnerability, and we were in it together now. They ended up staying the rest of the week, and we formed a true friendship. I'm sure that was a vacation they will never forget. It was as if it was written right out of an old western film.

Now, I wonder how the hell I imagined that I could keep it together to guide those people on their vacation when my own world was crumbling down around me again. Back then, I was sure of very little. But I knew this part of the land, this countryside, had raised me, as if the river had carved her way through my soul, and the peaks and the vast valley were lush with the wildlife who were akin to family for me. I knew that my horse would get me wherever I pointed her, her four strong legs holding me steady and her spirit bold and loving. I sought comfort in the red tail hawks flying above me as if Dad himself was leading the way with the wind gently pushing me ahead. If I could lean into this new world of the unknown, I would be taken care of. But I wasn't ready for this knowledge yet. More learning was needed, more growth, more breaking open.

Life at the ranch was very difficult after Dad's passing. We had a family meeting and concluded that we would continue to run the ranch as Dad would like. My sister Savanna and I took on the chore of managing. But with Dad now gone and Mother taking over, we had different visions. Mom didn't trust us and was being guided by outside counselors in what to do. These were some of my darkest days. Not only was Dad now gone, but my mother was listening to and being mentored by humans that weren't worthy of her faith in them.

I began drinking very heavily to cope. I had never really been a drinker. I had partied a little, dabbling

161

with it after leaving the Mormon church. Alcohol can be very enticing if you have been shooed away from it your whole life. I began drinking whenever I had to talk with Mother because I was so afraid of what I would say to her if I was sober. I drank to deal with the fifty guests who questioned me about Dad every day. I drank when I was overwhelmed by the thirty employees who were running amok.

I couldn't deal with the rage and anger I was feeling toward my mother, and it became apparent that the situation was unhealthy for all of us. I knew that if I stayed on at the ranch, I was no longer going to have a relationship with my mother, and I would be effectively orphaned. I was watching my father's dream become a circus of egos, including mine. My mother named a man who'd worked with us for years as the outfitter of record in Dad's stead, even though that previous fall, before he died, Dad had asked Rocky to start taking over this part of the business.

Mother did not honor these wishes. This was so painful, watching my mother care about, trust, and honor others before her own children. That broke me. I was irate. I could see the future of what was to come. I had worked with the man in question for most of my life. He was not respected, he did not work well with others, and he was lazy and egotistical. The very opposite of Rocky. I knew this was the start of the downward spiral of the life I had known at the ranch.

So I made the most difficult decision of my life. I stepped away from the ranch. It was an incredible mess,

162

laying down my swords, but I knew this was not a battle I was willing to fight. I had been here before with my lawsuit, facing lies from people I trusted who were deceiving me, and I could not do it again—I would not.

I went from seeking answers from Dad to searching for answers from God, from the universe, but I was too clouded by anger, alcohol, and grief to receive any clarity. One by one, my siblings tried to step in and help run the ranch, but they were all ultimately run off by the negativity, distrust, and egos that had become the ranch's driving force, the shit show that had become our father's legacy.

The ranch and its business slipped into a heavy quicksand, never really coming back to its days of glory. The greatest lesson I learned from all this was that it was not my dream to run the ranch, it was my father's. I had very deeply engrained principles of duty and integrity that kept me chained to the idea that I needed to do it for him. But that is the ego's way of taking hold—even my father's ego was taking hold of me.

You see, you can never live someone else's dream. You may think that you have served them and done well, but in time, you lose sight of your own dreams, your sense of self, and what you really want. Even if you have a similar dream, it will never be the same. You will never be able to be someone else in just the way they were. And the truth is, why would you want to? Why imitate someone else, follow someone else's dream, when there is a blank canvas in front of you, waiting to be splashed with incredible colors unique only to you?

The trivial matters of this earth are of no relevance to

163

those who have passed on. Through meditation, prayer, and seeking, I found peace in knowing that happiness, joy, and comfort are attributes of the spirit and are attainable here on this realm—but are secondary to the desires of the ego. A constant conversation, woven with conscientious thought, between ego and spirit must always be taking place, pushing and pulling you back to the trail of your truest, deepest desires.

Back to Nashville

After leaving the ranch, I decided to take another try at Nashville. I had some strong leads in the business, and I wasn't ready to give up the dream of being a successful recording artist. I kissed Rock goodbye, knowing we would be together again soon. With a fresh bag of new songs, heavy and deep from my life experiences, I made the 22-hour drive straight with a thermos of coffee, a truck load of vintage cowboy boots, and a desire for a new start.

Life and times hadn't changed much in Nashvegas, as the locals call it, since I'd last left. I got in quickly with record producers, writers, and artists. Playing around at local gigs, I sang my songs about Wyoming life, and I lined the front of the stage with the vintage cowboy boots I had collected and sold them along with my CDs. My vision was well-received, a cowgirl troubadour, and I got great attention and feedback.

I would sleep at friends' houses or in the back of my truck on the outskirts of town. Six weeks had passed, and I received an offer for a publishing contract even though I was still facing a legal issue to get out of my old contract. I was all set to go and sign them after a session with their other writers. I drove back to Music Row in my half-ton Chevy with the Wyoming plates and parked in front of a tall building bustling with humans. I made my way up to the top floor and down the hall to a starkly decorated office meeting room filled with six other aspiring songwriters.

We made our introductions and began the process of writing a new country hit, each human performing their little idiosyncrasies to begin the writing flow. Sitting with strangers in stiff chairs under hard fluorescent lights, loud horns and sirens blaring from the street below, I felt any inspiration I might have felt dry up.

My phone buzzed, and I excused myself from the group to check the message. I opened my phone to a beautiful picture of Rocky sitting on his white horse and looking up to the biggest, bluest Wyoming sky I had ever seen. The image pinged my heart hard. Here I was in a harshly lit office, trying to find inspiration about love and life, and a thousand miles away sat the love of my life in the most inspirational setting I'd ever known. My greatest loves and inspirations were gently nudging me, reminding me of all that truly mattered.

I quickly packed up my guitar, said my thank-yous to the group, and told them I had an urgent matter at home. I threw my guitar in the truck, hurried my way out of the parallel parking space, and drove. I drove all day and night, 22 exhausting hours, back to Wyoming. Back to campfire summer evenings, dirt road shenanigans, and lovemaking amidst the wildflowers. Back home to Wyoming. To golden plains wavering in the wind, with peaks of grandeur around each sneaky bend and fast-flowing rivers rich with wildlife. To a place where you can know everyone and no one. Where wild is not an ideal, but a verb.

This is my home. The lands that shaped me, the mountains that healed me, and the rivers that nourished me. Forests that gave space to my writings, melodies to my songs, and strength to my character. The place that raised the love of my life. My sweet Wyoming home.

CHAPTER ELEVEN:

Paper Bullets
of the Brain

Having decided to find my way as an artist from my home in Dubois, Wyoming, I learned that it took a lot of creativity to make a living. I made a vow to myself that I would receive money only from doing things that I loved and from my creativity. Instead of selling my cowboy boots from a stage, I did it at local rodeos and pop-up shops out of the back of my truck. It was lucrative, but I was itching for more.

Since I'd always been into western couture clothing, I decided to start a western clothing line with my friend Arnica. We called it Buffalo Valley Road, and the brand received a lot of attention after we were chosen as one of the artists for the 2010 Western Design Conference in Jackson and asked to design the clothing for Ms. Rodeo Wyoming's reign. What an exciting and fun way to create! The process of designing clothes and then bringing them to life was very rewarding, and I loved every minute of it.

I was also still supplementing my income singing at parties and wedding events, as well as deejaying at night. Life really seemed to be coming together. After two years of grief—first Dad passing, then, a year later, Rocky's father passing too—we were finally coming out of the heavy fog of mourning. Rocky's fence biz was taking off, and we were happy to be on an upward swing. The ranch was still operating under the same conditions as when I had left it. I would sometimes go out and help on special occasions, but mostly I was dedicated to my own projects

That Halloween, I was booked to deejay a local party. Deejaying was not something I loved, but it was an easy way to make money, especially in my off season of fall and winter. I had all the equipment and enough knowledge to make people dance and be happy.

One of the interesting things about being a performer or a deejay is that you are usually on a stage, elevated above the crowd, and have a wide perspective of the entire room. After a certain time of night (or certain number of drinks), patrons seem to forget that you're there. They act like they're shrouded by a cloak made of equal parts inebriation and bad choices. Frequently, I'd witness secret meetings, clandestine glances, and puking in the corner. One time, a dude looked me straight in the eye, whipped his penis out, and peed on the floor. Yep! Glory days. What I'm getting at is the veil of consequence gets really thin with loud music pounding, the alcohol flowing, and maybe a few illegal substances in the system.

I had not yet chosen total sobriety at this point in my life, but for some reason, I decided not to drink at all, not even a single glass of wine. It was unusual for me back then. I had an odd feeling, and my intuition had me on alert. My husband had been drinking beer, but not heavily.

By 3 a.m. the party had died down, and Rocky helped me gather the rest of the gear. As we opened the door outside, we were blasted with a biting wind—the thermometer read -11, which was unusually cold for the last part of October. We heard, from down at the other end of the lonely Main Street of our no-stop-sign town, loud yelling and scuffling. We saw headlights whipping around.

I was tired and done with drunk people. I wanted to start our 30-minute drive home. But Rocky wanted to go take a look. He climbed quickly into the passenger seat of our truck. "Hurry," he said. "I want to see if they need help."

I wanted no part of it. I told him at least four times that I wasn't going down there. But as we scoped out the scene from our car, we realized that we knew the two men brawling it out. When you live in a town of only 900 people, it's pretty easy to know just about everybody.

I turned our brand-new Dodge truck down Main Street and toward the scene. In the dead center of the four-lane road were two very drunk young men, duking it out. I had no idea why, nor did I care. Rocky, however, was persistent about helping them.

One of them, a man in his early to mid-thirties, was relatively new to town. His family, parents, and sister had brought their wealth with them, bought up a chunk of land, and hired several townspeople for their new construction projects, a sure way to generate excitement in such a small dot on the map. This battling man had a wife, two kids, and a striking smile. He'd been born in Sweden and raised in Australia. Between his affluence and his charming accent, he seemed like a motivated and fresh addition to the town.

My husband, a rather buff, big man himself, jumped out of the truck and pulled the men apart, telling the newcomer to get into our truck. While the other participant finally got in the truck with his wife and took off, I was not happy. As the Swedish man stumbled his drunk, inebriated ass into our truck with blood dripping from his face and knuckles, I crossly told him not to touch anything and that if he did, I'd drop him off in the nearest creek. I could smell the liquor heavy on his breath even from the driver's seat. I was furious.

As we drove, our drunken, unwanted passenger spieled gratitudes and slurry I-love-yous to both of us for helping him. We reached what we thought was his house—he hadn't been able to make it very clear where he lived.

Rock leaned over to me. "I better make sure he makes it in."

I was curt. "Hurry up."

Rock hefted the guy from the car to the front door about 100 yards away. The wind howling against our truck. Suddenly Rock came running back, yanked the door open, jumped in, and in the most intensely serious tone I'd ever heard from him said, "Drive! He said he was going to kill me."

I didn't hesitate. I was looking behind to back out of the driveway when I heard a thud on the hood. I whirled around to see. Leaning toward me from above the hood was the man, holding a pistol pointed right at my face.

I threw the gear into drive just as he let the first bullet loose.

It zinged loudly so close to my right ear that I could feel its heat on my cheek. My ears ringing and a rush of adrenaline sweeping my body, I sank as far down in the seat as I could. I couldn't see where I was driving.

Crack! Another bullet shattered the windshield and barely missed my head. My heart was pounding so heavily it felt like it was crushing my chest. I kept driving as four more bullets hit the truck, and kept going as I heard the last bullet fire. Even amidst the chaos, I had registered that his pistol looked like a Glock, and I counted six rounds shot off.

I was speeding in a neighborhood I didn't know. I was terrified I was going to slam into someone's home or garage, but I knew I had to GO. My eyes, my hair, and even my mouth were full of shards of glass. I didn't know if I'd been hit, or, honestly, if I was still alive. I was trying to scan my body for wounds, but I was so amped up on adrenaline, I couldn't be sure. I felt with my hands as best I could. No blood. Maybe all was well.

With a sickening thud, I flashed onto Rock and

hoped he hadn't been hit. *Oh, God. I can't lose him. These can't be our last moments together, my last words said.* As I drove crazily down the dark gravel street, my whole life with him flashed through my mind in a split-second: lovemaking on the bank of the Buffalo river, moonlit horseback rides, wild mountain pack trips, the pain we had both endured losing our fathers, our totally dysfunctional wedding, our unborn children. *Not now. Not today.*

I was so afraid I couldn't speak. While still driving frantically, I stretched my trembling hand across the console, completely unsure of what I'd find. Then his hand touched and squeezed it twice, like he always does when he wants a response. The most beautiful voice I've ever heard asked, "Are you hit?"

The warmth of relief flooded in, soothing my shaking body.

"No, are you?"

"I'm fine, are you hurt?"

"*No. Call the cops now.*"

We kept driving. Rock dialed 911 with one hand as he held my hand with the other so tightly that my fingers lost feeling. I started to come back into my body more, wiping the glass away from my hair and my clothes. I saw that our entire windshield was gone, and the chill of the air hit me now that the adrenaline surge was leveling out.

Rock was explaining our situation to dispatch when I passed a sheriff's truck. I began honking, flashing my lights, and even yelling at him. I saw his truck in our side mirror, whipping around to follow us. I pulled over. He pulled next to us, took a look at our truck, and said the only thing a rightful Wyoming officer should say: "What the hell happened to you two?"

We recapped the situation to him in as much detail as possible. I wanted the cop to hurry and apprehend this horrible man, as I was worried for the lives of his wife and children. What was he capable of doing to them? But Dubois is such a tiny town, there was no back-up for 100 miles. On this Halloween, the town's small police force was preoccupied with other drunken ordeals. So he was not apprehended until the next morning.

I had so much fear and uncertainty that night, I didn't want to go home. I was scared the Swedish man was going to follow us. I didn't want to go to the house of someone I loved in case he hurt them. I had lost the ability to see reason. We decided to go to Rocky's mother's house in Crowheart, feeling pretty secure we would be safe there. We knocked wildly on the door at three in the morning, frantically waiting for her to let us in, then started blurting out the incidents of the evening. As I spoke, I was shocked that this again was now becoming a bit part in my story.

Once again, I became the talk of the town, just like after my accident, after my very public and nasty court battle, and after my father's recent death—a photo of him in his casket had been on the front page. Being in a small town has its perks, but having your pain turned into fodder for local gossip hurts. You go to the coffee shop for a quick cup of joe, only to have every person in the place tell you what they would have done and what you should have done.

173

Having been through a harrowing experience or two, I can tell you that you never know how you are going to react until you are deep in the throes of any life-changing situation. No one truly understand how time stands still, or the way your body seems to get heavy. Or how you can feel paralyzed while everything happens around you at lightning speed. I had nightmares for weeks, if not months, of that man's bloody smile as he shot at me. I became very reclusive, although I was still performing publicly. I would go to events, smile, sing my songs, and get the job done. Then I'd go home, eat cake, and watch Netflix.

The man who shot at us fled the country before he knew even what the charges were against him. His parents got him out on bail, and by the way the prosecuting attorney treated us after that, I wouldn't be surprised to learn that some shady dealings went down. The family had written letters to all the business owners and to people of affluence all over town, apologizing for their son's behavior. We have not received an apology from him or his family to this day, but bump into them at almost every big social engagement, the grocery store, and the coffee shop.

My deep depression lasted for about nine months. I was experiencing PTSD, but I couldn't say it out loud or even articulate it to myself. I'd never been to war, so I didn't think I deserved those words. I had been shot in the face, but he missed—barely—so shouldn't I feel so lucky? I may have been lucky, but I still felt shame, fear, even guilt.

It was a long stretch of hard times. Rock and I grew distant from each other, dealing with the trauma in completely opposite ways. He worked and drank more; I cried and withdrew, hiding behind my performing persona. We drifted in and out of crying, staying positive, breaking down, getting back up.

One very late, wintery night, as I was driving home from doing shows in Jackson and on the same very long, lonely, dark street where we had picked up the shooter in Dubois, I saw some very odd tracks in the fresh laid snow. I slowed my truck down and followed the tracks to where they petered off outside a crusty bar. There, I came upon a bearded old man in the street, crying, screaming, and crawling, with no warm clothes on. I couldn't stop. Not with the recent shooting fresh in my heart. I yelled out the window as I passed, " I'll call for help!"

I was so ashamed of myself. I was so fucking angry at that stupid, selfish man who shot at me and shot away bits of my humanity. I pulled over only a couple hundred yards past the old man and turned on my hazard lights even though I knew that in Dubois at 2 am, no one else was driving around. I called the cops to come help this man and sat there in my vehicle, watching him from my rearview mirror as he writhed in alcohol-induced agony until the cops came.

His drinking was his pain. His actions spoke his pain. His suffering was clear in the tracks smeared across the street. Driving home, I felt deeply changed by the experience of witnessing his agony.

How much can one heart endure? I had often

pondered on this, especially concerning my own heart. Was I going to be able to pull up out of this last one? Trust again? Move forward again? Love myself again?

Several months after the shooting, my father came to me in a dream. He did not speak any words, but I saw him across the other side, on the banks of the Wind River. It was a beautiful summer day. I could see my father had something in his arms. I squinted to see what it was he had as he gently set down a little curly-haired blond boy beside him. Then, hand in hand , they started walking across the deep, wide river toward me.

At first, I was frightened. I didn't want them to get washed down river. But when I looked more closely, I saw that they were somehow only about ankle deep in the water. I was elated to see my father looking young, healthy, and vibrant. I couldn't wait for him to reach me, to hold me, to stretch his arms around me for a long hug.

As they got closer, my father picked up the little boy and handed him up the bank to me. As soon as I touched this sweet little boy, my chest broke open and a million shards of light burst out. I was blinded by the light. I could only feel incredible warmth and sheer joy. I pressed the little boy in closer to my chest, and I felt whole. When the light began to dim a little, I looked all over for Dad, but I could not find him. The river rushed by, and I was left on the banks with this incredible child.

I woke quickly. I was back in my bed, confused. My dream had been so real. For a split second, I couldn't tell dream from reality. I felt as though Dad had really been with me—and who was the beautiful child? Lying there in my bed, I soaked up the memory of the feelings I had experienced in my dream. I rolled over and told Rock about my dream and how wonderful it was to be with Dad. I told him of the little boy. He held my hand as I cried.

It wasn't even a month later that Rocky and I found out I was pregnant. I was scared and thrown off my game a little, until the flash of this dream came back to me and I once again saw my father with this little boy. Immediately my fear and anxieties were gone, and I knew that we were having a boy.

On March 22, 2012, Gideon Wayne (after my father's middle name) O'Neal was born to us. A beautiful little human sent to heal our hearts and to give me hope. The circle of healing light would continue through me.

In the following years, my mother had decided to sell the ranch. It was not a decision I wanted, or was comfortable with. Rocky and I fought hard to buy Triangle C from the rest of the family. There were tons of papers to fill out, hot emotions, and deep pain. It seemed like everything Rocky and I tried to do to make the ranch deal work fell through. I was at my wit's end. I desperately did not want to let my father down and allow his life's work to have been in vain, to let his legacy die along with him, but things were simply not working out.

By the time Gideon was around three years old, we had been living at the ranch, and the closing date of our deal was approaching I needed some answers, some guidance beyond my knowledge. I felt the tug from nature to come to her and get quiet, so I threw Giddy on my back, and we crossed the highway on foot and climbed up the face of what we called Mailbox Hill. We set off through the tall, sacred sagebrush onto an old logging road, stopping every 20 yards or so when Giddy would stop me and say, "Look, momma!" whether it was a chirping bird, a pine cone, or a common rock.

We came to a resting spot beneath a tall pine near my favorite quaky patch. I swooped Giddy down from my back and onto my lap as we both sat crisscross applesauce. I told Giddy to close his eyes and help me listen. Then I said a little prayer out loud: "Please help me. I'm confused what to do. Divine, help me see the right path. I need a sign. I need a very specific sign whether Rocky and I should buy the ranch. I'm too emotional. I'm too angry to make the right choice. Please help me. Dad, if you're here or near, I need your help too. Please show me."

Giddy sat very quietly between my legs as the wind picked up and the beautiful, strong scents of sage, pine, and dark earth enveloped us. I sat eagerly listening and waiting for a sign, but I heard only the wind whispering through the trees and a faint call from a magpie. I did feel more at peace as I opened my eyes, but I didn't feel any huge awakening.

I picked Gideon up from my lap, and as I set him in front of me, he bent over to pick up a beautiful wing feather of a red tail hawk. I had not seen it when we sat down. It was huge, and I wasn't sure how I could have missed it. Whenever I saw red tail hawks, I thought of Dad, and on days when I was missing him deeply, a soaring red tail hawk would always be near. I took this hawk feather as a sign that Dad had been near and was listening.

I scooped Giddy up onto my shoulders, and we made small talk about Dad as we ventured back to the ranch. We crossed the highway, and just as we stepped foot under the archway of the ranch's property line, a massive plume of smoke to the west, at the far end of the property, caught my eye. The plume was huge and getting bigger with every slight shift in the breeze.

I hurried to the main lodge, where employees and friends were already talking to the forest service, who was there scoping out the scene. A huge forest fire had started while we were out on our walk, and it was moving toward the ranch. I couldn't believe my eyes. We spent the next couple of days battling this fire, digging fire lines close to the buildings, weed-whacking, and mowing every square inch of earth we could to protect us.

We were finally forced off the ranch when the fire came so close you could throw a stone into it from the back deck. We were asked to gather our belongings, forced to choose in moments what were the most important items to keep and what could be replaced. As long as I had Gideon, Rocky, my guitar, and all our animals, I felt everything else could burn up with no regrets. We left the ranch in a mad hurry, watching in the rearview mirror as any shred of Dad that we had clung to was engulfed in a heavy cloud of smoke, a furnace of forest fire consuming all in its path.

After the fire died down and all the emotions that came with it were spent, I remembered my sacred ceremony on the mountain and the prayers I had asked. "Give me a sign," I'd prayed. I was humbled by the answer I'd received, and felt guilty that it took a natural disaster to get my attention.

The fire that had raged through our ranch changed everything. None of the buildings had burned down, but the fire had gotten so close it had scorched the side of many of them, and had raged through all the pastures and fence lines and left nothing but embers and dead standing remnants of the vast forest I had come to know from my many years adventuring on horseback. The scenery all around was shockingly different. It was a stark new landscape, a dark, eerie contrast from the lush green earth that I had known.

Somehow, it now was easier to let the ranch go. The fire had set a path for new life, new earth, and a fresh start. So we gracefully bowed out of our contract to buy the ranch, even though my heart was breaking. It was time to move on.

Serotinous is a scientific term for a seed in a pine cone that must be exposed to extreme heat in order for that seed to be able to be released. This is the only way a pine forest can regenerate—through the destructive path of fire. It seems devastating to witness, but it creates an opportunity for growth and change.

You see, we humans are not that removed from the natural world. We like to believe we are above it, that we have more control of our outcomes, more choice. But just like the seeds of the tall, dark pines, inside us we have the seeds of new life and new perspective, aching to be released. Only through enduring the heat of hell can we break open. The blaze of healing light continues through each of us who are willing to keep going.

180

Life doesn't stop, no matter the hurt you've seen. Even beyond the veil of consciousness we have influence. There are forces beyond our comprehension, guiding the circumstances. When my thoughts get heavy and things feel like too much of a burden, on days when I can barely walk and, looking down at my legs, I am reminded of all I have endured, I stop myself, get quiet, and change the narrative. I am blessed to have experienced it all. Because of all I've been through, I choose to live fully in every moment. There is no excuse for me. I've had too many close calls, too many second chances. I know without a shadow of a doubt that these trails have been mine to take. It is now the time to wake up and live.

Bullets, bones, horses, and ranches. Daddy's gone. This is the stuff of every Academy Award–winning western film. The western is a genre ripe with tragedy, glory, angels, cowboys, deceit, and resilience, set against sweeping vistas and accompanied by lilting soundtracks.

But this is not a film. There's no Oscar party to attend in glamorous clothing. No scripts, no angsty music to warn you of trouble ahead. This is the life of a woman, shattered yet determined. Limping beyond a grim prognosis and holding a battered, broken heart, seeking for gold to fill its cracks. No bullets can stop the force within. There are mountains to climb, valleys to plunge into growth. Over the next ridgeline will be more adventure and likely more pain, but in the end, this is an incredible story of a songstress cowgirl. You will know her by her grit and her songs of sorrow, love, and strength. She sings from atop the most beautiful steed.

If you squint, you can see me. I'm just over there. Riding off into the sunset.

Acknowledgments

Thank you, Rockstar, for being the man of my dreams, for holding me in the real world and allowing me to drop everything in our daily life to finish this book, and for walking me through the reliving of all of it. To my son Gideon for all the times I had to say, "No, I can't play— I have to finish my book." Thank you for being patient with me and for learning with me. To my mother and siblings: We are infinitely woven together for time and eternity. Thank you for growing with me. May this be a path for healing for all of us, for what we heal in ourselves now heals all the past and future generations. Thank you, Dad, for all the pain and all the glory. Thank you to Maggie McReynolds and her team for everything: wisdom, clarity, guidance, and, especially, patience with my computer skills. Thank you to Jenny Carr for continual support and inspiration, and to Ciela Winter for planting the seed. Finally, thank you to every piece of music that has moved me and to every horse that has carried me.

About the Author

Jess Camilla (Garnick) O'Neal is an award-winning singer-songwriter, fashion designer, author, director, actor, and horse lover. She lives in the wilds of Wyoming on the banks of the Wind River with her horses, dogs, hubby, and son, and gets all of her inspiration from these very things.

You can keep up with all of her shenanigans on all forms of social media **@jesscamillaoneal** and via her website, **jesscamillaoneal.com**.

Thank You

Dear beautiful reader,

Thank you for taking time out of this busy life to read this book. I'm truly and deeply grateful. I know that by sharing our voices and stories, we heal the broken vibrations inside of ourselves—thereby sending a healing shockwave to each human that we come in contact with. Thank you, thank you, you thank you.

As a gift from me to you, please go to
http://jesscamillaoneal.com/srwhtrack
for a free download of my song, "She Rides Wild Horses," which was the musical inspiration and short version of this book.

You can find me and follow me
on all social media platforms:

Instagram: @jesscamillaoneal
Facebook: Jessica Camilla Garnick O'Neal
Twitter: @neversweatjess
Snapchat: jesscamillaoneal

You can also find me on my website, jesscamillaoneal.com, where I post videos and new content frequently.

All of my music is available on iTunes, Amazon, Spotify, and SoundCloud.

CPSIA information can be obtained
at www.ICGtesting.com
Printed in the USA
FSHW020631160120
66064FS